Columba

Pilgrim and Penitent
597 - 1997

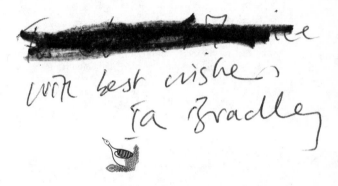

with best wishes
Ia Bradley

Ian Bradley

First published 1996

Wild Goose Publications
Unit 15, Six Harmony Row, Glasgow G51 3BA

Wild Goose Publications is the publishing division of the Iona
Community.
Scottish Charity No. SC003794. Limited Company Reg. No. SCO96243.

ISBN 0 947988 81 5

Cover design by Sarelle Reid
Front cover: painting of St Columba by Isabel Paul,
photographed by Peter Adamson

We gratefully acknowledge the contributions of:
THE DRUMMOND TRUST
3 PITT TERRACE, STIRLING
towards the publication costs of this book.

Distributed in Australia and New Zealand by Willow Connection Pty Ltd,
Unit 7A, 3-9 Kenneth Road, Manly Vale NSW 2093.

Permission to reproduce any part of this work in Australia or New Zealand
should be sought from Willow Connection.

A catalogue record for this book is available from the British Library.

Printed by The Cromwell Press Ltd, Melksham, Wilts.

'Columba of Iona is without question one of the great figures of the early history of Britain and Ireland. In the manysidedness of his character, so fierce and yet so compassionate, he shows us the power of Christ's gospel to bring healing and new life into a violent and disordered world. As we celebrate the fourteenth centenary of his death, we have the opportunity not just to make an historical commemoration but to enter anew into his heritage.

In this book, Ian Bradley does not disguise either the complexities of history or the challenges of the present. Rather through these things he points us to the continuing relevance of the vision of Columba with its mingling of prayer and politics, of praise, penitence and presence to the world's need. This is a vision which, as he tells us, has come to life again in many unexpected ways in the work and worship of the present Iona Community.'

(Review by Donald Allchin, writer and theologian)

For my mother, a daughter of Dál Riata,

whose stories of remote cells and retreats

on the coast of Kintyre

first fired my fascination with Columba.

Contents

Preface

Many sources have supplied and replenished the pure living water of Christian faith in the British Isles over the last one and a half millennia. Two particularly important streams began to flow in the period after the departure of the Romans, who were almost certainly the original bearers of Christianity to Britain, and brought the Gospel's refreshing and cleansing power to these islands more permanently. One had its source in Rome and entered England with St Augustine's mission to Kent. The other came from Ireland, although its original source was more likely Gaul or the Eastern Mediterranean, and entered Scotland with St Columba's journey to Iona.

It is a happy coincidence that in 1997 we are able to celebrate both these streams, it being the 1400th anniversary of St Augustine's arrival in Kent and of Columba's death on Iona. Each has contributed much to the Christian life and character of Britain, the Augustinian stream, flowing gently through the Anglo-Saxon and later the Anglican landscape, with its broad, eirenic tolerance, its spacious dignity and lofty language and its qualities of liberal moderation and sensitive pastoral concern, the Columban stream, coursing through the more rugged terrain of the Celts, with its fierce integrity and fervent enthusiasm, its austerity and asceticism and its theological questioning and disputatiousness.

All of us who are involved in the difficult but exhilarating enterprise of trying to live as Christians in Britain at the tail end of the twentieth century walk in the footsteps of these two great founding figures and carry something of their legacy. Both of them happen to have been particularly important in my own pilgrimage. Brought up in Kent, just a few stops down the railway line from the great Cathedral city of Canterbury where Augustine established his base, I came to faith and was confirmed in the chapel of Tonbridge School which is dedicated to him. Yet it was Columba who held a special fascination for me as a boy, perhaps because my mother had taken me back to her native Argyll to be baptised.

One of my most powerful childhood memories is of the picture of the saint in his cell on Iona which hung by the front door of our home. It is reproduced on the front cover of this book. Apparently the work of Isabel Paul, about whom I have been able to find out nothing, and exhibited in the Royal Academy in 1926, it depicts Columba sitting at his desk copying a psalm. At his feet are the crane whose flight to the island he prophesied to the monks and a sprig of oak possibly symbolising his pre-Christian druidic inheritance while in the background is the faithful white horse which came up to him and shed tears on the last day of his life. My father bought it as a present for my mother shortly before their wedding at St Columba's Church in London on 11 June 1949. I myself was married in the same church thirty-six years later. It was, therefore, a special privilege and pleasure to be asked by the Iona Community to write a short book on someone who had already played such a significant part in my own life.

It is, of course, all too easy to romanticize Columba, as the portrait which first caught my childish attention could be accused of doing. I have tried to avoid this temptation and to show the complex and essentially human character of someone who was a man as well as a saint. It is even more easy to romanticize what has come to be known as Celtic Christianity and find in its dim and misty essence all sorts of qualities which we feel are missing from church life today. Over the four years since I wrote my book *The Celtic Way* I have become increasingly conscious of this danger and increasingly uneasy about using the terms 'Celtic Christianity' or 'the Celtic Church'. For reasons which I explain at more length at the beginning of Chapter 4, I think it is more accurate and helpful to describe the subject matter of this book rather as 'Columban Christianity' or 'the Columban Church'. Even with these terms there is a danger of distortion. Yet, provided that we realise that we can never get back to the world inhabited by Columba and his successors, I believe that there is much that we can learn from them. It is not always a very comfortable message - certainly nothing like as instantly attractive as the package often presented as Celtic Christianity - but that does not make it any less important for us to heed today.

In preparing this book, I have incurred several debts. My principal thanks must go to the Iona Community for having the imagination to conceive of this project and the faith to commission me to carry out it out. I would especially like to thank Norman Shanks, the Community's leader, Sarelle Reid, Iona Macgregor and Nuala Feeney, respectively managing editor, project editor and publishing assistant of Wild Goose Publications, Peter Millar, warden of Iona Abbey where I spent a very rewarding couple of days, and John Bell, leader of the Wild Goose Resource and Worship Groups and a long-standing friend, who let me quote the hymn which he wrote with Graham Maule, 'From Erin's shores Columba came'. I have benefited from comments on an early draft of the typescript from Canon Donald Allchin and I am grateful to Betty Hannah for giving me permission to quote the hymn about Columba written by her late husband, John Hannah, to Oliver Davies and to SPCK, publishers of *Celtic Christian Spirituality; An Anthology of Medieval and Modern Sources* for letting me reproduce his translation of the poem which ends Chapter 4 and to Donald Meek for allowing me to quote from his forthcoming booklet on Highland religion. Extracts from *IONA: The Earliest Poetry of a Celtic Monastery* by Thomas Owen Clancy and Gilbert Markus are reproduced by permission of the authors and Edinburgh University Press, from Richard Sharpe's translation of Adomnan of Iona's *Life of St Columba* by permission of Penguin Books and from the World's Classics edition of Bede's *Ecclesiastical History of the English People* and Máire Herbert's *Iona, Kells and Derry* by permission of Oxford University Press.

A brief chronology of Columba's life

(All dates are approximate)

521   Born, possibly in Gartan, Donegal

561   Battle of Cúl Drebene between Northern and Southern Uí Néill

563   Leaves Ireland and comes to Scotland

574   Ordains Aédhán mac Gabhráin king of Scots Dál Riata

575   Attends convention of Druim Ceat

587   Founds monastery at Durrow

597   Death on Iona

The main sources for Columba's life and work

(In roughly chronological order)

Amra Choluimb Chille (The Elegy of Colum Cille) — probably written around 600 by Dallán Forgaill, an Irish poet.

Fo Réir Choluimb and *Tiugraind Beccáin* — two poems probably written around 650 by Beccán mac Luigdech, a hermit associated with the Iona community and possibly living on Rum.

The Irish Annals (especially those of Ulster and Tigernach) — chronicles recording events in Ireland which were started around the middle of the seventh century, possibly earlier. Some argue that a chronicle written on Iona and possibly started during Columba's lifetime, may underlie the earliest stratum of Irish Annals up to c.740.

Book of the Miracles of Columba — written probably in the 630s or 640s by Cummíne, seventh abbot of Iona, who died in 679. Only a tiny fragment of this survives.

Vita Columbae — the classic life written by Adomnan, eighth abbot of Iona, between 688 and 692.

Ecclesiastical History of the English People — written by the Venerable Bede in Jarrow and completed in 731.

The Irish Life of Columba — an Irish homily based on Genesis 12.1 and probably written in Derry around 1150.

1

The journey — pilgrimage, penitence or politics?

In or around the year 563 AD a middle-aged monk set off with a few companions in a small boat from the shores of his native Donegal, in the north west tip of Ireland, to brave the Atlantic swell. It is not clear whether he knew exactly where he was going nor how long he took to reach his ultimate destination which was to be the tiny island of Iona off the west coast of Scotland, about 100 miles away from his starting point. This journey is rightly perceived as one of the most significant events in the early history, and more particularly the early Christian history, of the British Isles. The monastery which Columba founded on Iona was to become one of the great spiritual powerhouses of early medieval Christendom, a beacon of Christian enlightenment and culture which shone brightly through the period which was for long described by historians with some justice as the Dark Ages. Iona became the base not just for the evangelization of much of modern Scotland but also, through its daughter foundation at Lindisfarne off the north Northumbrian coast, for large parts of northern and central England. Together with the other monasteries which Columba founded, it was also to play a key role in secular as well as ecclesiastical affairs, supporting the royal house which eventually provided the first rulers of the united kingdom of Scotland. Columba himself was to become a cult figure, venerated throughout Scotland and Ireland for his miraculous works, his sanctity and his protective powers.

Like so many aspects of his life and work, Columba's reason for leaving the comparative comfort and security of Ireland at the age of forty-one to start a new life in a much wilder and less hospitable region is unclear and has been the subject of much speculation and controversy. Modern psychologists might well see it in terms of a classic mid-life crisis in which a man approaching middle age and bored with his conventional existence seeks a new challenge. Yet there is nothing to suggest that Columba had become fed up with life in Ireland where he seems to have been deeply involved in monastic life and also to have taken an active interest in political affairs. Others might point to the sense of 'wanderlust' in the Celtic temperament which has led so many Irish and Scots to leave their native shores. Having reached Iona, however, he seems to have settled there and not to have done any more travelling, apart from occasional visits back to Ireland on political and ecclesiastical business and periodic forays into the Scottish Highlands and Islands. He did not have the restless spirit of other notable Irish saints, like his contemporaries Brendan of Clonfert, who journeyed far across the Atlantic, and Columbanus who set off from his monastery in Bangor around 590 for a lengthy progress across Europe.

Modern evangelical Christians might be inclined to relate Columba's journey to Iona to a conversion experience. It certainly seems to have marked a turning point in his life and one recent secular historian has used the language of conversion to explain this change of direction. Alfred Smyth writes of this episode: 'We seem to be dealing with a classic conversion story, involving not necessarily the conversion of a great sinner to repentance, but the giving at least of a new intensity to a life already dedicated to the church. For Columba, like Paul, or even like Christ or Mohammed, seems to have waited to translate his fervent sense of mission into action when he reached middle age, and from then on his life took a radically new direction'.[1] Yet there is no evidence that he did, in fact, undergo any kind of dramatic religious experience prior to his departure from Ireland. Unlike Patrick, who according to his own confession was called in a vision to evangelize the Irish, Columba is not portrayed by any of his biographers as having received a direct call from God to cross the sea to Pictland and evangelize its heathen inhabitants. Indeed, as we shall see, there is some doubt as to whether he saw himself as a missionary at all. Nor did the nature of his life change quite as much after 563 as some commentators have suggested. On and around Iona in the last thirty-four years of his life, he seems to have gone on doing the same kind of things that he had been involved in during the first forty or so in Ireland — praying, copying manuscripts, offering pastoral care and spiritual leadership, founding and running monastic communities and playing a high-profile role in the dynastic disputes and political rivalries of Irish and British kings and chieftains.

Perhaps it is to Columba's near contemporaries that we should turn for an explanation as to what motivated his fateful journey to Iona. Their writings about him have a very different perspective from those of modern commentators and emphasize two of the most important themes in what has, for better or worse, come to be known as Celtic Christianity — pilgrimage and penitence. Both of these themes derive from the essentially monastic culture of early Irish Christianity and its stress on asceticism and holiness, self-discipline and sacrifice. The early sources convey a sense that Columba made his journey from Ireland to Iona as a pilgrim and a penitent. They suggest that there was both a voluntary and perhaps also an enforced element in his exile from his beloved native land and that in setting off for Scotland he may have been atoning for some misdemeanour, as well as renouncing the comfort and security of home.

The briefest and most factual account of the journey comes from the pen of Adomnan, Abbot of Iona from 679 to 704: 'In the second year following the battle of *Cúl Drebene*, when he was forty-two, Columba sailed away from Ireland to Britain, choosing to be a pilgrim for Christ'.[2] The concept of *peregrinatio* (the Latin word which Columba and his contemporaries used) was very different from pilgrimage as we think of it today. It was not a matter of going off to particular holy places and experiencing a spiritual buzz or 'high' there. For the early Irish monks pilgrimage was rather a perpetual exile from the comforts and distractions of the world. It was, indeed, a way of bearing witness to Christ and a kind of martyrdom in which Christians separated themselves from all that they loved for the sake of God. Pilgrimage had clear penitential overtones: it was often undertaken at the instigation of a soul-friend or confessor with the object of purging the individual *peregrinus* of worldly attachments and affections.

Pilgrimage of this kind had a particular appeal to Columba's fellow countrymen. In the words of the historian Thomas Charles-Edwards, '*peregrinatio* was the most intelligible form of ascetic renunciation available to Irishmen'.[3] This was because of the strength of family ties and landed wealth, the importance of local patriotism and the legal bars to travel which were such marked features of early medieval Irish society. There was also a clear scriptural basis behind this desire for exile and pilgrimage. In the Gospels Jesus repeatedly calls on those who would follow him to leave home and family. Perhaps an even more direct influence on the Irish *peregrini* was the Old Testament narrative of the journey of the people of Israel through the wilderness and across the desert. God's words to Abraham, 'Leave your own country, your kin, and your father's house' (Genesis 12.1) were often quoted in connection with the journeys undertaken by Irish monks. Indeed, they provided the inspiration for the mid-twelfth century Irish *Life of Columba* which took the form of an extended meditation on this particular text. It was not, however, towards a land flowing with milk and honey that many Irish *peregrini* felt led. Rather they sought out desolate, isolated, barren places where they stayed for a while in caves or cells before moving on again. Another influence was important here — the example of the Egyptian desert fathers like St Antony who had established a pattern of discipleship based on withdrawal from the world and solitary contemplation.[4]

Columba's journey in 563 does not seem to have involved quite such a radical act of discipleship as was made by the desert fathers. He did not opt for the solitary life himself, although he may well have spent substantial periods living alone in cells around the west coast of Scotland after moving to Iona and he certainly encouraged the practice of the eremitical or solitary life in his monastic foundations. Yet if he was not to cut himself off from human companionship and worldly concerns, his journey from Ireland does seem to have involved an element of exile, whether voluntary or imposed. This impression is reinforced by the admittedly unsubstantiated tradition that he first landed on Oronsay but found that he could still see Ireland from there. So he went on further to Iona and climbed the highest hill. It was only after satisfying himself that he could no longer see his beloved homeland and erecting a cairn which now gives the hill its name — *Carn Cúil ri Erenn* (the cairn of Back towards Ireland) — that he settled there. In a sense he had both physically and metaphorically cut himself off from his native land, although he did return there at least twice, in 575 and 585.

Several of the poems written about Columba in the century or so after his death portray his journey from Ireland as both an epic adventure and an act of purgation and self-denial. These two elements are particularly marked in the poems attributed to Beccán mac Luigdech, a hermit associated with the Iona community who possibly resided on the island of Rum in the mid-seventh century. One of them dramatically evokes the power of the Atlantic swell into which Columba and his companions launched themselves:

> *In scores of curraghs with an army of wretches*
> *he crossed the long-haired sea.*
> *He crossed the wave-strewn wild region,*
> *foam-flecked, seal-filled,*
> *Savage, bounding, seething, white-tipped, pleasing,*
> *doleful.*[5]

Another of the poems attributed to Beccán, '*Fo Réir Choluimb*' (Bound to Columba) pursues this imagery of the ocean's wildness to suggest that Columba is purging himself:

> *He crucified — not for crimes —*
> *his body on the grey waves ...*
> *He left Ireland, made a pact,*
> *he crossed in ships the whale's shrine.*
> *He shattered lusts — it shone on him —*
> *a bold man over the sea's ridge.*[6]

Beccán, it will be noted, goes out of his way to emphasize that Columba's self-sacrificial journey was not made in any way to atone for crimes. Several historians, however, have drawn a rather different conclusion on the basis of remarks made in Adomnan's life and in the *Annals of Ulster*. They have suggested that Columba's departure from Ireland may have been forced on him as a way of either atoning for or escaping from the consequences of some crime or misdemeanour in which he had been involved. Of key importance to this interpretation is the battle of Cúl Drebene mentioned by Adomnan as having taken place two years before Columba's voyage. This battle, which took place near Sligo, was one of the most important skirmishes in a long and bloody struggle between two powerful dynasties for control of Ireland. It reminds us that Columba's era was an age of warlords as well as saints. Ireland at this time was made up of around 150 *túaths* or small kingships, each with fierce tribal and clan loyalty to their ruler. Over them was the *rí Temro*, or high king of Ireland. This position was claimed by the Uí Néill, the family from which Columba himself came, but it was disputed between their northern and southern branches.

In the battle of Cúl Drebene in 561 the ruler of the Southern Uí Néill, Diarmait mac Cerbaill, sometimes described as the last of the Irish high kings to reign from the pagan sanctuary of Tara, was decisively defeated by a coalition led by the King of Connaught and members of the northern Uí Néill, among whom were Columba's first cousin and his uncle. According to the *Annals of Tigernach* the victors 'prevailed through the prayers of Columba' which miraculously drove away a mist conjured by pagan priests to conceal Diarmait's advancing army. Several historians have suggested that it was not just prayers that Columba offered to his kinsmen and that he may also have taken part in the fighting. There are several pieces of evidence for this. According to Adomnan, Columba had a 'livid scar, which remained on his side all the days of his life'. Was this the result of a wound sustained at Cúl Drebene or at some other fracas between the northern Uí Néill and their traditional rivals? Adomnan also writes of Columba being excommunicated from the church for certain 'trivial and pardonable' offences and being made to appear at a synod held at Teltown in County Meath. Those convening the Synod apparently dropped the charges against Columba after evidence was brought of supernatural signs of his favour in the eyes of God. Adomnan seems to have concluded the chapter in which he described this event with the statement: 'During this period St Columba crossed to Britain with twelve disciples as his fellow soldiers.'[7]

It is tempting to draw the conclusion from this evidence that Columba's departure from Ireland was bound up with his censure by the Synod of Teltown and may well have been imposed on him as a penance and a condition for his return to the church. But what was the offence for which he was excommunicated and for which he may have been forced to leave his native shores? Was it his involvement in the battle of Cúl Drebene or was it rather, as Adomnan implies, something more 'trivial and pardonable'? A possible answer to this question, which exonerates Columba from direct involvement in the battle but links into the dynastic rivalry between the northern and southern Uí Néills, lies in the oft-repeated story of the illegally copied psalter.

Tradition has it that the offence for which Columba found himself hauled before the Synod of Teltown involved the unauthorized copying of a beautiful book of psalms which St Finnian had brought back from Rome and placed in the church of his monastery at Moville in County Down. Columba is said to have stolen into the church late at night some time in the year 560 and in some versions of the story he is accused of having taken away the psalter and failed to return it. Finnian apparently appealed to his protector and high king, Diarmait mac Cerbaill, who censured Columba and demanded the book's return and the surrender of the copy he had made. Columba refused at least this second request and was backed by his northern Uí Néill cousins who were spoiling for a fight with their arch-rival Diarmait. In some accounts this incident is portrayed as sparking off the battle of Cúl Drebene. The story is not totally beyond the bounds of credulity. We know how deeply attached Columba was to the Book of Psalms and how much of his time was spent copying psalters. There is a tradition that Columba underwent part of his monastic training under Finnian at Moville, which had been founded in 540, and it is therefore not inconceivable that he could have been back there as a fully professed monk. It seems curious and uncharacteristic, however, that he did not seek permission before copying the psalter. What may be more significant is the link made between Columba and the bloodshed at Cúl Drebene. Whether the incident involving the psalter is true or not, the impression given by the various versions of this story is that the Saint carried a certain responsibility for the battle between the northern and southern Uí Néills and had blood on his hands. Later sources suggest that Columba felt a deep sense of remorse and willingly accepted the penance of life-long exile from Ireland as an atonement for his sins.

The question of Columba's involvement in the battle of Cúl Drebene is a matter of debate among historians and it is important to point out that several regard it as a complete red herring in terms of the reasons for his journey. However, whether there was anything to it or not, it highlights the importance of his royal blood and aristocratic connections. If he had not opted for the monastic life, or had it chosen for him by his parents, Columba would almost certainly have been ruler of a *túath* and might well have been high king of Ireland. His great grandfather had been the half-legendary Niall of the Nine Hostages, a pagan king who raided Roman Britain and gave his name to the Uí Néill warlords. His particular branch of the family, the Cenél Conaill, rose to power over the Uí Néills as a whole in 566, five years after the Battle of Cúl Drebene and three years after his departure from Ireland, when his first cousin, Ainmere mac Sétnai, became high king. The dynasty of Cenél Conaill survived as one of the main royal houses of Ireland until the seventeenth century.

In one of the most recent and detailed academic studies of this period, Máire Herbert suggests that it was Columba's royal connections that prompted his journey from Ireland to Iona in a spirit of pilgrimage. Dismissing the notion that his departure was linked either with the battle of Cúl Drebene or the Teltown Synod, she writes: 'One may suppose that the Uí Néill churchman perceived that his family connections made it difficult for him to remain apart from the public arena, and to pursue the ideals of monasticism. Therefore, as renunciation of wealth and claims to kingship in Ireland no longer seemed to suffice as ascetic ideals, he sought a *potioris peregrinationis locus* overseas.'[8]

Columba's royal connections could point to quite another reason for his journey to Iona. He may have gone to help consolidate the new Irish kingdom being established across the sea and to forge close links between its rulers and the northern Uí Néill. In making the perilous crossing from Ulster to the west coast of Scotland, he was following in the wake of a substantial number of his countrymen. These Irish migrants (known by their Roman name of *Scoti*) came particularly from the *túath* or kingdom of Dál Riata in Antrim. By the time of Columba's birth (which is generally dated to around 521) enough of them had settled in their new homes to form the nucleus of a second kingdom of Dál Riata whose boundaries corresponded with the modern region of Argyll. As abbot of Iona, Columba was to be instrumental in building up the power of the rulers of this new Scottish kingdom and in forging a close alliance between them and his own northern Uí Néill kinsmen in Ulster. It is conceivable that he went there initially either at the behest of the king of Scots Dál Riata or of his own royal relatives for largely political reasons.

There are conflicting accounts of where Columba's journey from Ireland in 563 first took him. Some sources suggest that he went first to Dunadd, the stronghold of the king of Dál Riata which was situated on a rocky hill one mile north of Kilmichael Glassary in North Knapdale on the Kintyre peninsula. Here he is said to have met and talked with the king, Conall mac Comgaill. Adomnan writes of such a meeting taking place two years after the battle of Cúl Drebene although he does not specify where it took place. *The Annals of Ulster* speak of Conall, who ruled Scots Dál Riata from roughly 559 until his death in 574, granting the island of Iona to Columba as a gift. Some historians argue that the saint did not, in fact, move to Iona until 574, more than ten years after his departure from Ireland, having spent the interim period on the unidentified island of Hinba (variously identified as Jura, Colonsay or one of the small Garvellach islands south of Mull) where he is known to have founded a monastery. One possible reason for this delay is the suggestion that at the time of his initial journey from Ireland Iona was still in the hands of the native (and pagan) Picts. A further complication is provided by the Venerable Bede who states twice in his *Ecclesiastical History of the English Speaking People* that it was, in fact, the Picts who gave Iona to Columba. However, this is generally regarded as unlikely. It may be that the island was still under Pictish control when Columba arrived from Ireland but it seems most likely that it was the king of Dál Riata, Conall mac Comgaill, who gave it to him as a site for his new monastery, even if Irish rule over the island had to be established before he could take up residence there.

I have dwelt at some length on the confusing and ultimately unresolved question of exactly why Columba came to Iona for two specific reasons quite apart from its intrinsic interest. Firstly, it alerts us to the enormous difficulty of disentangling fact from legend and shows the degree to which the sources for the Saint's life are scanty and confusing. Secondly, it introduces the dominant features that made up Columba's complex character — part pilgrim, part penitent and part politician. This was not a man who spent the first half of his life in worldly pleasure and the second half in saintly seclusion. His life had much more consistency and much more variety. The Saint of Iona remained very much the diplomat and power-broker, dabbling in dynastic politics and sometimes acting like a proud warlord while at the same time spending hours in prayer, meticulously copying psalms, grinding corn and washing the feet of his monks.

If this suggests a split personality, then it is certainly true that Columba's character, in so far as we can discern it through the layers of legend and veneration that have built up over the centuries, displays a number of contradictions. He never lost the attributes of the warrior aristocracy into which he had been born and retained to the end of his life an autocratic imperiousness, a hasty temper, a fierce pride and a lingering attachment to the 'fascinating rattle of a complicated battle'. Yet he could also be gentle, humble and overflowing with Christian charity. This juxtaposition is perhaps the basis for the tradition which appears in some later sources that he had two names: first *Crimthann* (the fox) and later *Columcille* (the dove of the church). It is just conceivable that the earlier name may reflect pagan origins and that he acquired the second on being baptized as a Christian but this must be conjecture. The characteristics of both the fox and the dove continued to manifest themselves throughout his life. They are well captured in a hymn to commemorate Columba written by John Hannah, a priest in the Scottish Episcopal Church who died in 1984. It was included in the (sadly) little used *Hymnal for Scotland* [9] which appeared in 1950:

> *Who is this so fierce and warlike,*
> *Slow to mercy, swift to chide?*
> *See him rouse the clans to battle*
> *To avenge his wounded pride.*
> *'Tis the crafty warrior, Crimthann,*
> *Spreading hatred far and wide.*
> *Evil passions seek to brand him,*
> *And his maker's image hide.*
> *Who is this so strong and gentle,*
> *Rich in prayer and wise in lore?*
> *See, the very beasts befriend him*
> *As he walks Iona's shore!*
>
> *'Tis Columba, saint and abbot,*
> *With the Cross the Saviour bore;*
> *He proclaims throughout our homeland*
> *Holy Gospel's wondrous store.*

If we are to encounter the true Columba, we need to acknowledge this ambiguity and to come face to face with Crimthann as well as Columcille. This was no plaster saint but an intensely human figure with faults and weaknesses as well as extraordinary depths of gentleness and humility. For his biographer, Ian Finlay, 'there is nothing inconsistent in believing Columba was both a truly great Christian evangelist and teacher and also an ambitious and resolute statesman. Nor is there any reason why he should not have been tender, devoted, angelic, and yet passionate, irascible and, on occasion, even ruthless in achieving his ends. The Celtic temperament runs to extremes.'[10]

Alongside the excesses of the Celtic psyche, we can perhaps point to another feature of the outlook of the early Irish monks to help explain one aspect of what might seem a double life. They understood the basic rhythm of Christian life and the need to balance activity in the world with withdrawal from it. The ideal of *peregrinatio* involved a certain degree of exile, renunciation and searching for one's own desert place of resurrection. Except for those few called permanently to the solitary eremitical life of the anchorite, however, it did not mean a complete withdrawal from the world and its affairs. The monastic life was far from being one of retreat and escape. Indeed, monasteries were almost certainly the busiest institutions in Celtic society, constantly teeming with people and fulfilling the roles of school, library, hospital, guest house, arts centre and mission station. Most of the great Celtic saints alternated between periods of intense activity and involvement in administrative affairs with lengthy spells of quiet reflection and months spent alone in a cell on a remote island or rocky promontory. In this, they were following the example of their Lord and Saviour, one moment surrounded by crowds and engaged in preaching, teaching and healing, and the next walking alone by the lakeside or engaged in quiet prayer in the mountains.

Columba's life exemplified this balanced rhythm. At times he was busily engaged in founding monasteries, negotiating with kings, attending councils, going on missionary journeys and ruling his ever-expanding monastic *familia*. Yet his biographers also portray him spending long periods praying or copying the Scriptures in his cell and he frequently took himself to Hinba for solitary retreats. In many ways this combination of action and meditation provided a perfect example of what modern theologians call 'praxis' — a combination of involvement in practical issues and theological reflection on them. In the words of a poem written about him just a year or two after his death, 'What he conceived keeping vigil, by action he ascertained.'[11]

To a considerable extent these two sides of Columba's character were the product of his noble birth and monastic training. He mixed as easily with warlords and princes as with monks and scholars. Through his veins coursed the blood of a long line of fierce pagan warriors. It would hardly be surprising if this element in his make-up sometimes came to the surface and caused him to do things which he may have later regretted. His upbringing, however, was entirely monastic. From a very early age he seems to have been destined for the church and he spent his boyhood and teenage years being tutored by priests in monastic foundations. This in itself was not particularly unusual. The children of the Irish warrior aristocracy were generally fostered out to tutors for their education and sixty years or so before Columba's birth Patrick noted in his *Confession* that 'sons and daughters of Scottic chieftains are seen to become monks and virgins for Christ'.[12] Columba probably belonged to the sixth or seventh generation which had known Christianity in Ireland. By 431 the Christian community on the island was large enough for the Pope to send out a bishop called Palladius to oversee it. Some years later Patrick began his work of evangelization which seems to have spread across much of the country. He is generally credited with giving the church in Ireland an organized diocesan structure although within a generation of his death in or around 493 this seems to have broken down and the dominant institution in Irish Christianity had become the monastery.

The middle years of the sixth century saw the founding of several of the great monastic houses in Ireland which were to dominate the Christian landscape of the island for the next five hundred years. Among them were Moville, set up by Finnian in 540, and Clonmacnoise, established by Ciarán in 548. This was the world in which Columba grew up and received his training. We know tantalizingly little about his early life. Adomnan reports that as a boy he was brought up by an elderly priest called Cruithnechan. Later and less reliable sources tell of him learning the alphabet by eating shaped biscuits and remembering the one hundredth psalm when his ancient teacher forgot it. Subsequently he seems to have studied at a monastery in Leinster, which had one of the best-established church schools in the first half of the sixth century, and possibly at Moville. The Irish *Life of Columba*, composed around 1150, states that he completed his training under another Finnian at Clonard and, having been ordained presbyter, joined a monastic community near Dublin. After a plague there, he apparently returned to his own Cenél Conaill people in Ulster where he may have founded some small monastic communities. Later sources claim that he set up some three hundred monasteries in Ireland before his departure from Iona including the communities at Derry, Raphoe, Durrow, Kells, Lambay and Moone but this is generally dismissed by historians as without any historical basis. The truth is that we do not know where Columba was based or what he was doing before he made his fateful journey from Donegal in 563. What we do know is that he was an exceedingly well-connected monk who had something of the qualities of both the fox and the dove in his complex character. To find out more about this fascinating and enigmatic figure we need to turn to the record of what he did when he came to Iona.

Notes

1   Alfred Smyth, *Warlords and Holy Men* (Edward Arnold, London, 1984), p.9
2   Adomnan of Iona, *Life of St Columba*, translated and with an introduction by Richard Sharpe (Penguin Books, Harmondsworth, 1995), p.105
3   Thomas Charles-Edwards, 'The social background to Irish *peregrinatio*' in *Celtica*, no.11 (1976), p.56
4   On this important group of Christians, whose influence on Irish monasticism was very considerable, see *The Lives of the Desert Fathers* introduced by Benedicta Ward and translated by Norman Russell (Mowbray, Oxford, 1981)
5   Thomas Clancy and Gilbert Markus, *IONA The Earliest Poetry of a Celtic Monastery* (Edinburgh University Press, Edinburgh, 1995), p.147
6   *Ibid.*, p.136
7   Adomnan of Iona, *op.cit.*, p.208. See note 356 to the Penguin edition for a discussion of the placing of this remark in Adomnan's original text
8   Máire Herbert, *Iona, Kells and Derry* (Clarendon Press, Oxford, 1988), p.28
9   *Hymnal for Scotland incorporating the English Hymnal and Authorized for Use in the Episcopal Church of Scotland* (Oxford University Press, Oxford, 1950)
10 Ian Finlay, *Columba* (Victor Gollancz, London, 1979), p.187
11 Thomas Clancy and Gilbert Markus, *op.cit*, p.113
12 John Ryan, *Irish Monasticism* (Four Courts Press, Dublin, 1992), p.91

2

Columba the man —
king maker and church planter

Two activities dominate Columba's public life as it is portrayed in
the earliest surviving accounts — forging relationships with kings
and establishing a network of churches and monasteries. The
prominence of these two themes in early sources may throw more
light on the preoccupations of Columba's biographers in the century or so following his death than on the Saint's own priorities.
Recent scholarship has clearly demonstrated that Adomnan deliberately cast his subject in the role of Samuel and stressed
Columba's king-making activities in order to support the claim
of later Iona abbots to consecrate the kings of Dál Riata. It is also
clear that the twelfth-century Irish *Life* portrayed him as setting
up numerous monastic foundations in Ireland as part of its attempt to assert the primacy of Derry over the Columban *familia*.
Yet even allowing for exaggeration and special pleading on the
part of his early biographers, it is impossible to ignore the considerable evidence they provide that both king making and church
planting ranked high on Columba's own agenda.

If these seem somewhat incompatible occupations, then we are
brought back to the tension that we have already identified within
Columba's personality. The gentle, scholarly monk who periodi-
cally retreated to his cell and spent the night reciting psalms on
the sea shore was also the high-born friend of kings who involved
himself in political affairs. The man of God was also a man of
action. Columba's deep commitment to following Christ and to
the monastic and priestly vocation did not efface his loyalty and
blood-ties to his Uí Néill and Cenél Conaill kinsmen. Nor did it

quell his fascination with the dynastic disputes of the day.
Adomnan's life is full of prophecies about the outcome of battles

and predictions as to who would succeed to a particular kingship. Although several may not be genuine it is difficult to dismiss them all and to avoid the impression that they give of a man whose life had two distinct focuses — the one spiritual and centred on the institution of the monastery, the other secular and centred on the institution of kingship.

In fact, these two themes were much more compatible and intertwined than might at first sight appear. Columba almost certainly used his royal connections to forward the cause of Christianity and to win powerful support and patronage for the church. He also seems to have been more than happy to provide Christian legitimation for kingship and to offer prayer and protection both to his royal kinsmen and to other princes and monarchs. The way in which he bound the two relatively new institutions of church and monarchy together was to have profound and positive implications for the future development of both and for the order and stability of early medieval British society. In the opinion of the distinguished contemporary historian of early Ireland, Máire Herbert, 'overall, perhaps the most important aspect of the achievement of Colum Cille was the fact that he bridged the divide between secular and ecclesiastic realms of interest. More than that, his career may be seen to have shown the potential for mutual benefit arising out of co-operation between church and dynasty.'[1]

Columba lived at a time of transition when the anarchy of a society dominated by tribal warlords was giving way to a more peaceful and settled system of government based on rule by a number of royal dynasties. This movement towards greater order was both paralleled and helped by the development of monastic confederations which often enjoyed close relations with the emerging royal households and shared their territorial boundaries. As we shall see, the Columban *familia*, which consisted of the monasteries founded both by Columba himself and by his successors, was to become easily the biggest and most influential of these confederations, its fortunes closely linked with those of both the Northern Irish Uí Néill and the rulers of Scots Dál Riata.

The close connection between the development of the institutions of church and monarchy in the period from the sixth to the tenth century is important to understanding the nature of Christianity in the Celtic realms of the British Isles. It made a significant mark on the poems and prayers of the time which often took up the language and imagery of kingship in their depiction of God and Christ. A notable example occurs in the eighth-century Irish poem, *'Rob tu mo bhiole, a Comdi cride'*, known to us through its early twentieth-century translation and versification as the hymn 'Be Thou My Vision' which twice refers to God as 'the High King of Heaven'. It was not just in Celtic Britain, of course, that kingship and Christianity progressed together and that royal patronage helped the cause of the church. The apparent conversion of the Emperor Constantine in 312 and the subsequent promotion of Christianity as the favoured religion in the Roman Empire had led to a great increase in church building and ecclesiastical wealth and influence in Continental Europe, possibly at the expense of the integrity and simplicity of the earlier followers of Jesus. Within the British Isles there seems to have been less ostentatious building up of ecclesiastical establishments. That is not to say, however, that the support and patronage of secular rulers was any less important to the church. An appreciation of this fact was no doubt partly what made Columba so keen not just to keep in with kings but to help them on their way.

The way in which Columba built up close relations with rulers is highlighted in the friendship which he apparently established soon after his arrival from Ireland with the king of Scots Dál Riata, Conall mac Comgaill. As we have already noted, some sources suggest that Columba made Conall's stronghold at Dunadd on the Kintyre peninsula his first port of call and that the king gave him the island of Iona for his monastic foundation. There are also grounds for thinking that Columba's Uí Néill relatives may have encouraged him to go and settle in Scots Dál Riata in order to promote an alliance with the rulers of this potentially powerful new kingdom. Whatever its origins, there is no doubt that the close relationship forged between Columba and Conall proved mutually beneficial to their successors. It ensured royal patronage and protection for the church centred on Iona while greatly enhancing the prestige and legitimacy of the new Irish kingdom in Scotland. For the next two hundred years or more the fortunes of the Columban monastic *familia* and the royal house of Dál Riata were inextricably intertwined.

There is an interesting confirmation of the closeness of this link and an intriguing glimpse of Columba as kingmaker in Dál Riata in the one surviving fragment of the life of him written by Cummíne, the seventh abbot of Iona, in the 630s or 640s. It tells of the Saint promising the kingship to Conall's cousin, Aedán mac Gabhráin, and his descendants on condition that they are loyal to his successors as abbots of Iona and his royal kinsmen in Ireland. In his slightly later *Life* Adomnan devotes a chapter to this episode, describing an angel of the Lord visiting Columba when he was on the island of Hinba and commanding him to ordain Aedán as king. The Saint is at first reluctant to follow this order, preferring Aedán's brother Eoganán, but the angel strikes him with a whip (the origin, according to Adomnan, of the scar which remains with him for the rest of his life) and returns on three successive nights to repeat the demand that Aedán must be ordained king, a ceremony which Columba duly carries out on his return to Iona where he finds Aedán waiting for him.

Adomnan's description of what appears to be a fully-developed royal anointing ritual is the first of its kind in European literature and has led some historians to suggest that the first recorded Christian ordination of a king anywhere in Europe took place on Iona in 574. An important recent monograph has, however, cast doubt on the historicity of this event. Michael Enright has suggested that the episode of Aedán's ordination may have been invented by Adomnan and inserted in his *Life of Columba* in order to bolster the concept of Christian kingship in general and more specifically to support the claim of the abbots of Iona to consecrate the kings of Dál Riata.[2] It is certainly true that Adomnan makes much of Columba's role in choosing as well as anointing the rulers of Dál Riata. He is portrayed as picking out under divine inspiration both Aedán and his successor Eochaid Buide. Both Enright and Dr Richard Sharpe, editor of the latest edition of Adomnan's life, agree that the chapter which describes the Saint's choosing of Eochaid Bude is directly based on the Old Testament story of Samuel choosing David to replace King Saul.[3] It may well be that Adomnan over-emphasized Columba's king-making activities for his own purposes and projected back an arrangement which had only developed in his own time whereby the abbots of Iona consecrated the rulers of Dál Riata in order to give it greater authority and tradition. This should not, however, lead us to lose sight of the importance of the link between the spread of Christianity and the legitimization of kingship in Celtic society, nor of the key role that Columba's successors on Iona, if not the Saint himself, played in strengthening that link.

Columba's apparent close interest in the fortunes of kings and princes was not just confined to those in his adopted Scottish homeland. He also continued to maintain close contact with his royal relations back in Ireland. Indeed, he may well have been the moving spirit behind a convention held at Druim Ceat near Derry in 575 which brought together the northern Uí Néill and the rulers of Scots Dál Riata. The leading representatives of each group, Aed mac Ainmirech, King of Cenél Conaill, and Aedán mac Gabráin, King of Dál Riata, were both figures with whom he had very close connections. Columba himself was apparently present at this gathering which seems to have cemented the alliance between these two powerful dynasties and had the effect of making Scots Dál Riata independent of its Irish counterpart. According to the poet Dallán Forgaill, the Saint came to the convention more in the guise of a Celtic chieftain than a humble monk, bringing with him a retinue of forty priests, twenty bishops, fifty deacons and thirty students. Ian Finlay comments: 'As a Celtic prince, he would be aware that a meek appearance would count for nothing and that he must present himself with a semblance of the trappings of royalty'.[4]

There is also evidence that Columba made it his business to forge good relations with the kings of the principal peoples who occupied the Scottish mainland in the sixth century. As in Ireland, this was an important period of transition in which the anarchy and territorial warfare that had followed the departure of the Romans around 400 gave a way to a more settled situation where the country was broadly split up between four separate kingdoms. While the Irish (known by their Roman name of *Scoti*) increasingly dominated Argyll and the Inner and Outer Hebrides, south west and west central Scotland were inhabited by the Strathclyde Britons, whose king was based in Dumbarton. The Highlands, the north east and east central Scotland was the heartland of the Picts, whose high king ruled from Inverness. The Lothians and Borders were part of the Anglian kingdom of Bernicia and were effectively ruled by the kings of Northumbria.

Columba seems to have had dealings with the rulers of all four of these groups which would eventually be brought together under a single monarch to form the modern nation of Scotland. He was naturally closest to the kings of Dál Riata who were of Irish ancestry like himself, in alliance with his own Uí Néill kinsmen and in control of the area where he established his monasteries. He is also portrayed as being on cordial terms with Roderc, king of the Strathclyde Britons, who seems to have been a Christian. Although there is no direct evidence of contact with the rulers of Bernicia, the fact that two Northumbrian princes fled to Iona for sanctuary in 616 suggests that relations between the Columban *familia* and the Northumbrian royal family must have been established either during the Saint's lifetime or very shortly after it.

Perhaps the most interesting and also the most inscrutable of Columba's royal relationships was that with Brude, the Pictish king. The sources are frankly conflicting here. Bede seems to suggest that Columba converted the pagan king to Christianity eight years after he had become ruler of his people (i.e. in 566) and that it was as a consequence of this conversion that Brude granted the Saint the island of Iona which was under Pictish control. This, however, seems a less likely account of their dealings than that contained in Adomnan's *Life* which describes at least one encounter between the two men at Brude's stronghold near Inverness but makes no claim that the pagan king was converted to Christianity. Indeed, Adomnan does not portray Columba as setting out to convert Brude or the Picts and gives a much more limited purpose to the Saint's journey through the Great Glen to confer with the pagan king, suggesting that its primary object was to secure royal protection and safety for a group of monks from Iona who were living as hermits on Orkney. It is also possible that there may have been a political agenda behind the meeting of Columba and Brude with the Pictish king being anxious to secure an alliance with the Dál Riata Scots at a time when he was anxious about the rising power of the Anglian kingdom of Northumbria.

Were Columba's dealings with kings and princes motivated by his penchant for mixing with monarchs and political parleying and his enthusiasm for the institution of kingship or by his evangelistic zeal and desire to open up new mission fields for the Iona monks? Behind this question lies the much bigger issue of whether Columba was primarily an ecclesiastical administrator or a missionary. Were the last thirty-five years of his life spent largely on Iona building up and administering the monastery and its satellites or were they rather filled with preaching tours and missionary journeys around Scotland and perhaps even further afield?

Once again, the evidence is conflicting. Some sources portray Columba in the years after 563 as largely remaining on Iona and dividing his time between priestly and pastoral duties, scholarly pursuits and the leadership of the monastic community. This is broadly the picture given by Adomnan although his *Life* records the Saint making frequent trips to Hinba, possibly for regular periods of solitary retreat, and also visits to Skye and Ardnamurchan. On a number of occasions Adomnan describes Columba as journeying to the other side of Druim Alban ('the Spine of Scotland' and thought to refer to the Grampian Mountains) and being among the Picts. There is, in fact, considerable debate among scholars as to how many journeys into Pictish territory Adomnan reports Columba as making. Some are inclined to put the number as high as seven although Marjorie Anderson, editor of an important edition of Adomnan's *Life* which first came out in 1961, takes the view that all of his accounts relate to one single expedition made up the Great Glen to Brude's court. Although Adomnan describes a number of individual conversions secured by Columba on his travels, the overall impression is not of missionary activity and certainly not of mass evangelism.

Other sources make much more of Columba's missionary endeavours and portray him as being constantly on the move, converting the heathen people of North Britain. The Irish *Life* perhaps conveys this impression most strongly: 'When Colum Cille had founded Iona he went on a preaching circuit among the Scots and Britons and Saxons, and converted them to faith and belief after he had performed many miracles and raised the dead to life'.[5] The *'Amra Choluimb Chille'* suggests more specifically that his main missionary field lay among the Picts in central and eastern Scotland (modern Angus and Perthshire), describing him as 'the teacher who would teach the tribes of the Tay' and commenting that:

> His blessing turned them, the mouth of the fierce ones
> Who lived on the Tay, to the will of the king.[6]

The most quoted passage about Columba's missionary activities, and its antecedents, comes from Bede's Ecclesiastical History:

In the year of our Lord 565 ... there came from Ireland to Britain a priest and abbot named Columba, a true monk in life no less than in habit; he came to Britain to preach the word of God to the kingdoms of the northern Picts which are separated from the southern part of their land by steep and rugged mountains. The southern Picts who live on this side of the mountains had, so it is said, long ago given up the errors of idolatry and received the true faith through the preaching of the Word by that most reverend and holy man Bishop Ninian, a Briton who had received orthodox instruction at Rome in the faith and the mysteries of the truth. His episcopal see is celebrated for its church, dedicated to St Martin, where his body rests, together with those of many other saints ... This place which is in the kingdom of Bernicia is commonly called Whithorn, the White House, because Ninian built a church of stone there, using a method unusual among the Britons.[7]

Bede's words, which were written at least one hundred years after Columba's death, have been highly influential in determining the popular impression of how Scotland was evangelized. They suggest that Columba was responsible for bringing Christianity to the northern Picts — those living in the northern and western Highlands and in Aberdeenshire north of the Mounth (the upland ridge which skirts the Dee Valley from Lochnagar to Aberdeen), the southern Picts, inhabiting Perthshire, Angus, Fife and the lands around the Forth, having earlier been converted by Ninian, a shadowy figure for whom our only sources, apart from Bede, are an eighth-century poem and a twelfth-century *Life* by Ailred of Rievaulx. As a result of Bede's account, Columba and Ninian have posthumously vied for the accolade of being hailed as the true apostle of Scotland. Scholars have championed one or the other in a somewhat unedifying academic wrangle which has often owed more to sectarian prejudices and ecclesiastical partisanship than to the interests of historical truth. Columba has found favour with enthusiasts for all things Celtic and with those who have seen him as establishing a proto-Presbyterian church clearly distinguishable from the episcopally governed church favoured by the Rome-educated Bishop Ninian. Ninian's champions, on the other hand, have been drawn particularly from those with an anti-Irish agenda who have wanted to stress the Britishness of the native Galloway saint and emphasize the indigenous nature of early missionary activity in Scotland.

The debate over which saint should be seen as the principal evangelist of Scotland was particularly lively in the early decades of this century. Leading the pro-Columban camp was William Watson, Professor of Celtic at Edinburgh University who underlined the Irish contribution in the Christianizing of Scotland and enthusiastically followed Bede in crediting the conversion of the northern Picts to Columba. Ranged against him were a trio of Protestant scholars, Frank Knight, United Free Church minister and keen archaeologist, Archibald Scott, Church of Scotland minister in Kildonan (Helmsdale) and Dr Douglas Simpson, librarian of the University of Aberdeen. Knight pointed to the large number of evangelists active in Scotland prior to Columba. Scott was in no doubt as to the primacy of 'Ninian the Great' over Columba and regarded the 'great mission' undertaken by the Briton as the key event in the early Christian history of Scotland, leading directly to the establishment of what was to remain the sole church of the Picts until the time of Kenneth MacAlpin in the mid-ninth century.[8] Douglas Simpson was even more enthusiastic in his championship of Ninian and his dismissal of Columba. Holding that the Irish saint's political activities were 'consistently directed against the Pictish King and people', he held that 'long before Columba's time, Christianity was widely spread among the Picts'.[9] The key agent of this early evangelization of Highland and northern Scotland had to be Ninian. On the basis of church dedications, Simpson argued that the British saint had travelled from Galloway via Glasgow and Stirling to Dunottar and Methlick in the north east and Glenurquhart in the Highlands. In his view, indeed, Ninian got as far north as Caithness and Shetland.

More recent and less partisan scholarship has seriously challenged, if not completely exploded, the arguments of Scott and Simpson and has suggested a much more limited role for Ninian. Charles Thomas, Professor of Archaeology at Leicester and one of the leading contemporary authorities on Christianity in Britain in the period between 300 and 700, has cast grave doubts on Simpson's assertions about the extent of Ninian's travels by demonstrating that many of the church dedications which he took to be contemporary were in fact made several centuries after the

Saint's death.[10] In a recent book John MacQueen, former Director of the School of Scottish Studies at Edinburgh University, has argued that Ninian was largely active in the areas of Dumfries, Bernicia (the Borders) and possibly in Renfrewshire and Stirling and that he did not penetrate significantly into areas occupied by the Picts.[11] Archaeological finds tend to support this theory in that there is no evidence for Christianity among the Picts until the sixth century at the very earliest.

The dating of Ninian and the nature of the church with which he was involved have also been the subject of considerable controversy over the last few years. There is uncertainty as to how soon after the departure of the Romans from Britain he appeared on the scene and whether the church in Galloway of which he appears to have been a bishop, with its centre at Whithorn, was a surviving offshoot of Roman Christianity, possibly linked to ecclesiastical centres further south such as Carlisle or even York, or an early example of indigenous British Christianity.

We know from archaeological evidence that a Christian settlement existed at Whithorn at least from the mid-fifth century, making it an earlier eccliesiastical and monastic site than Iona. The Latinus stone, which apparently marks the grave of a father and daughter, at Whithorn, which was found there can be dated to this period and is, in fact, the earliest Christian memorial in Scotland. What is not clear, even from Bede's account, is whether Ninian actually founded the church at Whithorn, nor how long before Columba he lived. Previously it was thought that Ninian was a contemporary of Martin of Tours, the Hungarian-born saint who brought Eastern monasticism to the West and who died in 397. This date was traditionally taken for the foundation of Whithorn, largely on the basis of a remark in Ailred's *Life* that news came through of Martin's death as the church there was being built. This gave rise to the idea that Ninian had visited St Martin's monastery in Gaul on the way back from his training and ordination in Rome and dedicated his own monastic foundation to him when he returned to his native Galloway in the last days of Roman occupation of Britain.

Modern scholars are almost all of the view that this is too early a dating for Ninian. John MacQueen places him in the first half of the fifth century while still holding on to the traditional view that he founded the church at Whithorn. However, a more recent and highly persuasive article by the Glasgow-based scholar, Dr Alan Macquarrie, argues that Ninian almost certainly belonged to the first half of the sixth century and as such overlapped with Columba. In his view Whithorn was already a thriving monastery and Christian centre when Ninian, who had been born around 493 from the same British Christian stock as Patrick, went there to train. He possibly travelled to Rome, coming back to Britain as a missionary bishop working predominantly south of the Forth, notably in the Borders area around Peebles. Possibly he later returned to Whithorn as Bishop of Galloway, rebuilding the church there and dedicating it to St Martin of Tours, whose cult seems to have been strong among north British Christians. Several early sources mention Ninian as coming into conflict with Tudwal, a king of Dumbarton, whose reign Macquarrie reckons can be dated fairly accurately to the mid-sixth century. On this interpretation, Ninian died around 563, just thirty years or so before Columba. Like Dr MacQueen and other modern scholars, Dr Macquarrie is convinced that Ninian did not venture beyond southern Scotland. If he did do any preaching or evangelistic work among the Pictish people, then it was with an extreme southern offshoot who lived south of the Forth.[12]

If this recent work somewhat diminishes the importance and primacy of Ninian, it does not necessarily establish Columba as the unchallenged apostle of Scotland and chief evangelist of the Picts. Rather it places both men in the context of a more gradual and fragmented process of Christianization in which many others also took part. The Ninian versus Columba debate has at least produced one beneficial result in reminding us that there were two different movements at work bringing Christianity to seventh-century Scotland. The older one came from the British church, centred possibly on Carlisle and with its missionary base in Strathclyde, sending missionaries westwards into Dumfries and Galloway, eastwards into the Northumbrian controlled Lothians, northwards towards Stirling and possibly into the Pictish lands of Perthshire and Fife. The other more recent missionary movement came in the wake of the Irish push into western Scotland and spread from its base in Dál Riata westwards into the central Highlands and Tayside and north into the Highlands and the north east. Place names can give us much information as to the progress of these two movements. Names with 'eccles' (deriving from the

Latin *ecclesia* and the British *eglwys*) suggest early Christian churches founded under British influence. They are found in considerable numbers across southern Scotland, with a particular concentration in the south west, and up the east coast between the Forth and the Mounth but are hardly found north of the Mounth or west of the Great Glen. Other place names give evidence of early Irish penetration — a good example is Atholl in north Perthshire which derives from *Ath Flhóda*, meaning 'a second Ireland'.

The extent to which these two movements had their early headquarters at Whithorn and Iona respectively is by no means certain. Although Bede states that 'Iona was for a very long time chief among all the monasteries of the northern Irish and the Picts' there is little evidence that Columba himself planted any monastic communities or churches in the Pictish regions of Perthshire, the Highlands and the north and north east.[13] Bede's remarks probably apply to the period a hundred years or more after the Saint's death when his followers had established communities in Pictish territory and possibly also when churches founded by missionaries not associated with Iona had become absorbed into the increasingly powerful Columban *familia*. It may well be, in fact, that there was a third important movement bringing Christianity to the Picts in the late sixth and early seventh century quite independent of the British mission from Whithorn and the Irish mission from Iona. The conversion of those who lived in the region of the Tay may well have been brought about by monks and nuns based at Abernethy, near Perth. The origins of the monastery there, from which the fine round tower still survives, are shrouded in mystery and it is not clear whether it was founded by British or Irish evangelists, or even as an indigenous Pictish initiative. Three of the lists of Pictish kings assign the foundation of Abernethy to 463, which would conceivably make it earlier than both Whithorn and Iona, but others put it later. Most scholars are inclined to opt for a date during the reign of either Gartnait, who died around 601, or Nechtan, who ruled in the 620s. This later dating is probably the most likely. There is a tradition that Nechtan founded a church dedicated to St Brigit at Abernethy in the presence of Darlugdach, abbess of Kildare. Alfred Smyth has suggested that Nechtan also ruled Strathclyde and that he may have founded the house with Irish nuns from Kildare around 625. Whenever it was established, and whether its first members were Irish, British or

Picts, there is no doubt that the monastery at Abernethy played a very important role in the evangelization of Perthshire, Fife and Tayside from at least the early seventh century onwards. I have heard it argued very persuasively that Abernethy rather than Iona should be regarded as the true cradle of Christianity in Scotland but that is not a claim which I think I had better pursue in a book commissioned and published by the Iona Community!

Columba was by no means the only Christian missionary, if, indeed, missionary he was, to be active in the vast areas of central and northern Scotland which were occupied by the Picts in the sixth century. Nor was he the first to penetrate these pagan realms. In his seminal two volume study of the archaeological evidence for the early Christianizing of Scotland Frank Knight identified eighty men and women who were actively evangelizing the country before Columba had left his native Ireland and 'who had literally covered the land with hundreds of churches before the Iona Mission began'.[14] It is difficult to avoid the conclusion that had they been fortunate enough to have royal blood, find a biographer like Adomnan and forge close links with the family that was to provide Scotland with its ruling dynasty, they too might have become famous names.

Among these early pioneers were several near-contemporaries of Columba who came from Ireland, and established monasteries in Dál Riata. St Catan, St Moluag and St Blane all hailed from the monastery at Bangor in County Down. Catan founded a community at Kilchattan Bay at the south end of Bute and was possibly also associated with foundations on Colonsay, Islay and Jura. Moluag founded an important monastery at Lismore before working in the Hebrides, notably on Skye and Tiree, and then moving to the north west, where he died possibly at Rosemarkie in Ross-shire in 592. Blane is traditionally credited with establishing the church at Dunblane after first setting up a monastery at Kingarth on Bute. According to some accounts St Machar, associated with preaching to the Picts of Aberdeenshire and founding the church and city of Aberdeen, was one of Columba's original companions on his journey from Donegal. Another of his original companions, if an equally unlikely story is to be believed, was St Donnan, who seems to have evangelized much of Skye and who became one of the first Christian martyrs in Scotland when Pictish raiders massacred all 150 members of the community that he had established on the island of Eigg in 617.

Curiously, Adomnan makes no reference in his *Life* to any of these Irish monks despite the fact that they were apparently living and working so close to Iona. However, he does refer to Columba's friendship with a number of others who seem to have been operating quite independently of Iona and its daughter foundations. In one chapter he describes 'four saints who had founded monasteries in Ireland' visiting Columba on Hinba.[15] Significantly, two of them seem also to have established monastic communities in Scotland although Adomnan does not mention these, presumably out of a concern not to detract from the primacy of the Columban *familia*. St Comgall of Bangor seems to have set up a monastery on Tiree and St Brendan of Clonfert at Eileach an Naoimh in the Garvellochs in the mouth of the Firth of Lorne. The other two Irish saints described as making the visit to Hinba were St Cainnech of Aghaboe and St Cormac, who is also portrayed by Adomnan as being commended by Columba to King Brude and voyaging to Orkney. This reference has led some scholars to suggest that Columba 'sub-contracted' evangelistic work among the Picts, especially those in the northern isles, to Cormac.

A number of other Irish and British monks were also preaching to the Picts during Columba's lifetime. They included St Kessog, who supposedly evangelized the Trossachs from his base on Monk's Island in Loch Lomond, and St Serf who seems to have been active in the Ochil hills and Fife and had a similar island retreat on Loch Leven. St Ternan, a shadowy figure possibly based at Abernethy, is associated with the Christianizing of the Dee valley in Aberdeenshire. St Columba's best-known evangelist contemporary, the British-born St Kentigern, is traditionally portrayed as the first bishop of the Strathclyde Britons. He did most of his missionary work in Strathclyde although an almost certainly fabricated story in Jocelyn's twelfth-century *Life* describes him meeting Columba near the banks of the Tay. There were undoubtedly many other monks whose pioneering work in bringing Christianity to the remoter parts of Scotland has gone unsung while their better-connected contemporary continues to receive honour and attention. Dr Alexander McBain, a distinguished expert in the study of the Gaelic language, noted more than a hundred years ago that Columba 'swallowed up into his own fame all the work of his predecessors, companions and contemporaries, and deprived generations of pioneers and missionaries of their just fame'.[16]

It certainly seems on the basis of the best available evidence we now have that Columba does not deserve the accolade of apostle to the Picts. His forays into Pictish territory seem to have been few and far between and it is highly doubtful that he felt any evangelistic impulse to convert this particular people to Christianity. Instead his missionary efforts, such as they were, seem to have been concentrated almost entirely among the *Scoti* in Dál Riata. Although Adomnan describes him as founding monasteries on both sides of Druim Alban, i.e. among the Irish and the Picts, there is no evidence of any Columban foundations in areas occupied by the Picts and all those that we know of are either in Scots Dál Riata or Ireland. It seems likely that Columba's missionary work among the Picts was confined to isolated individual instances of conversion and baptism of the kind described by Adomnan. More concerted evangelism almost certainly did not come until the seventh century when it was undertaken by such figures as St Maelrubha, a possible relative of Columba who lived from c.642 to 722 and made a series of journeys from his base at Applecross into Inverness-shire, Banffshire, Skye and Harris, and as far north as Cape Wrath. Archaeological evidence suggesting that the area around the Moray Firth was not converted to Christianity until the late seventh or early eighth century would certainly tend to favour Maelrubha, rather than his better known predecessor from Iona, as the true evangelist of the northern Picts.

How then should Columba's part in the story of the Christianizing of the British Isles be assessed? Perhaps we should follow his early biographers and regard him less as a missionary or evangelist and more as a planter of churches. This is certainly how Adomnan saw him. In the second preface to his *Life* he describes Columba as 'the father and founder of monasteries'. The elegy that appeared a few years after his death refers to him as *cét cell custóit* (the guardian of a hundred churches). This may be an exaggeration but there seems little doubt that he was personally responsible for founding a number of monasteries. In Scotland, apart from Iona, these included communities on Tiree, Hinba, the island of Elen (which has been tentatively identified by Sally Foster as Jura) and on the shores of Loch Awe. Significantly all of them lie within the kingdom of Dál Riata. There is also strong evidence that he returned from Iona to Ireland to found a monastery at Durrow around 587. Columba almost certainly established other communities in Ireland, notably at Derry which may well have served as a port of communication between Iona and his monasteries in Ulster.

Ian Finlay has written that 'monasteries seem to spring up and bloom like flowers in the footsteps of Columba, as though he created them with a wave of his *bachuil*; but we know that in the first place he had to negotiate with the king of the tribe for the grant of the land on which to build his "city", then for endowments with which to launch and maintain it.'[17] Here is a link between the two main activities which seemed to occupy Columba's public life, at least if his early biographers are to be believed. There are other connections between his king-making and church-planting activities. He ran his monasteries as though they were a kingdom, grouping them into a *familia*, or federation, bound together by ties of kinship and establishing a dynasty to rule over them with himself as the first high king. Again and again, Columba seems to have planted a monastic community in some remote spot and put one of his relatives in charge of it. His uncle was abbot at Hinba, his first cousin at Tiree and the son of another cousin at Durrow. Significantly in the century after his death all but one of the abbots of Iona, who exercised overlordship over the entire Columban *familia*, were close blood relations of the founder. In the words of Máire Hebert: 'The manner in which Colum Cille organized the government of his monastic foundations would seem to have been based on established secular concepts of overlordship, kinship and inheritance, so that the system had an in-built potential for survival and continuity in Irish society'.[18]

As abbot of Iona Columba behaved very much like an Irish high-king. Although assiduous in caring for the souls and bodies of the members of his own monastic *familia*, the evidence suggests that he could also be fiercely autocratic and jealously territorial when it came to dealing with those outside it. He seems, for example, to have sought to prevent monks from Whithorn from setting up a community in the Hebrides, regarding such a move as an unwarrantable intrusion into his own sphere of influence. His authority derived as much, if not more, from his own personal charisma and leadership qualities than from his office. This reflects William Leask's dictum that 'the Celtic race is prone to follow leaders and not institutions'.[19] It was also undoubtedly helped by the significant power that abbots were coming to wield in the Irish church, itself another consequence of the close link between the spread of Christianity and the development of kingship. As Kathleen Hughes, the leading historian of early Irish Christianity, has written, 'The bishop stood in a similar relationship to his diocese as did the petty king to his *túath*; but the head of a great monastic *paruchia* was like a king over kings'.[20] The author of a recent study of early Irish monasticism, Hugh Connolly, comments in similar vein: 'The abbot became the administrative head of the Church and was often referred to as a *princeps*. He became the centre of power in a loose, disaggregated system, which had at its base the great monastic family'.[21]

The word 'family' suggests close ties of kinship, loyalty, community and solidarity. It is significant that the Irish word for family is *muintir* which derives from the Latin *monasterium*. For Columba both the individual monastic community and the wider monastic federation were first and foremost families over which he presided as a benevolent, if firm, founding father. The same was true of the *túath* ruled by a just and kindly king. In his king making and his church planting, Columba was seeking to bring the order, stability and community of family life into the political and religious spheres. In place of the arbitrary rule of warlords and chieftains, he championed a new kind of authority in which the exercise of legitimate power and strength was tempered and complemented by the Christian virtues of justice, humility and mercy. These are the very qualities which, by all accounts, he brought to the oversight of the monasteries which made up his own extended family and which formed a kingdom which was firmly rooted in this world and yet also pointed to the world beyond.

Notes

1 Máire Herbert, *op.cit.*, p. 35
2 Michael Enright, *Iona, Tara and Soissons: The Origins of the Royal Anointing Ritual* (Walter de Gruyter, Berlin, 1985)
3 See Richard Sharpe's note no.358 in Adomnan of Iona, *op.cit.*, p.355
4 Ian Finlay, *Columba*, p.154
5 Máire Herbert, *Iona, Kells and Derry*, p.261
6 Thomas Clancy and Gilbert Markus, *IONA*, pp.111, 113
7 Bede, *The Ecclesiastical History of the English People* (Oxford University Press, Oxford, 1994), pp.114-15
8 Archibald Scott, *The Pictish Nation: Its People and Its Church* (T.N. Foulis, Edinburgh, 1918), p.1.

9   W. Douglas Simpson, *The Historical Saint Columba* (Milne & Hutchison, Aberdeen, 1927), p.1. Simpson's thesis can also be found in his books *The Celtic Church in Scotland* (Aberdeen, 1935) and *St Ninian and the Origins of the Christian Church in Scotland* (Edinburgh, 1940) and his pamphlet *On Certain Saints and Professor Watson* (Aberdeen, 1928).

10   Charles Thomas, 'The Evidence for North Britain' in *Christianity in Britain, 300-700* edited by M.W. Barley and R. P. C. Hanson (Leicester University Press, Leicester, 1968), pp.94-116

11   John MacQueen, *St Nynia* (Polygon, Edinburgh, 1990)

12   Alan Macquarrie, 'The Date of St Ninian's Mission: A Reappraisal' in *Records of the Scottish Church History Society* vol.XXIII, Part 1 (1987)

13   Bede, *op cit.*, p. 114

14   G. Frank Knight, *Archaeological Light on the Early Christianising of Scotland* (James Clarke, London, 1933), p.7

15   Adomnan of Iona, *op.cit.*, Book Three, Chapter 17

16   Quoted in J. D. Galbraith, *St Machar's Cathedral: the Celtic Antecedents* (Friends of St Machar's Cathedral, Aberdeen, 1982), p.1

17   Ian Finlay, *op.cit.*, p.81

18   Máire Herbert, *op.cit.*, p.35

19   W. K. Leask, *Dr Thomas McLauchlan* (Oliphant, Anderson & Ferrier, Edinburgh, 1905), p.168

20   Kathleen Hughes, *The Church in Early Irish Society* (Methuen, London, 1966), p.74

21   Hugh Connolly, *The Irish Penitentials* (Four Courts Press, Dublin, 1995), p 9-10

3

Columba the Saint — priest and poet

So far I have not mentioned the feature which dominates all the early writings about Columba — his sanctity as exemplified in a life filled with prophesying, miracle working and heavenly visions. This aspect is particularly evident in Adomnan's *Life* which is almost wholly devoted to the Saint's supernatural qualities, its three books covering respectively his prophetic revelations, his miracles of power and his visions of angels. His sanctity also figures prominently in the other major sources for Columba's life. The account written by Cummíne, seventh abbot of Iona, forty or so years after the Saint's death, and now largely lost, was significantly entitled *The Book of the Miracles of Columba*. Descriptions of supernatural signs and wonders also abound in the poems and eulogies written about him in the seventh century by Dallán Forgaill and Beccán mac Luigdech.

This aspect of Columba's life, as it has been presented to us by his near contemporaries, causes considerable difficulties to the modern post-Enlightenment Protestant mind. The eighth Duke of Argyll, who was instrumental in restoring Iona Abbey in the 1890s and making it available once again for Christian worship on an ecumenical basis, found it impossible to cope with 'the atmosphere of miracle' pervading Adomnan's life which he rejected as 'childish and utterly incredible'.[1] He was forced to the conclusion that the author had resorted to deliberate invention. Many other modern readers must have similar reactions as they encounter stories of the fearless and versatile Saint taking on the Loch Ness monster, driving out a devil that was hiding at the bottom of a milk-pail and making a stone float in water like an apple.

Yet if we are to engage with and understand the culture which shaped Columba, and perhaps even more the outlook of those who followed him, we have to come to terms with a concept of sainthood which is very different from that which prevails today and which will strike many modern minds as primitive and credulous. As Thomas Owen Clancy and Gilbert Markus have commented, 'It is the belief in saints which separates, more than anything else, the medieval world from the classical world which preceded it, and the modern world which followed it'.[2] Nowadays, sainthood either has very technical connotations in terms of the various hoops through which those proposed for canonization in the Roman Catholic Church posthumously have to jump, or else it is associated primarily with qualities of humility, gentleness, forbearance and kindness which make us say of someone that she or he is 'a real saint'. In Columba's day, not just in the Celtic world but throughout Christendom, it was part and parcel of a cult of holy men and women whose sanctity was effectively demonstrated and proved by their ability to make prophecies and work miracles as much as by their inner qualities of discipline and self-sacrifice.

It is in this context that we need to approach the lives of Columba written by Cummíne and Adomnan and the poems by Dallán and Beccán. They stand in an early Christian tradition of *Vitae Sancti*, or saints' lives, which are essentially works of hagiography rather than biography, being designed to depict their subjects as exemplars of holiness, aiming not at historical accuracy and impartiality but at building up their readers' faith. Among the earliest and most important of these *Vitae* was Athanasius' *Life* of St Antony of Egypt, the pioneer desert father, and Sulpicius Severus' *Life* of St Martin of Tours, the figure who brought the principles of eastern monasticism to the west. Both of these works heavily influenced Adomnan's treatment of the life of Columba and he quoted verbatim from the latter at a number of points in his own book.

The clearest influence on this particular genre of early Christian literature are the Gospel stories about the life and work of Jesus. The authors of the *Vitae Sancti* sought to establish the saintliness of their subjects by showing how closely they followed in the footsteps of their Lord. This involved portraying them as working miracles as well as taking up their own crosses and following the path of self-denial. Several of the wonders which Adomnan depicts Columba performing — turning water into wine, stilling a storm, raising a dead boy to life and driving out demons — directly parallel miracle stories in the Gospels. Others, such as the drawing of water from the side of a hard rock, recall episodes in the Old Testament. There are also clear Biblical echoes in the 'Annunciation' passages found in all the early *Lives* of Columba which describe the Saint's birth being foretold by a series of signs and wonders.

There is another substantial clutch of miracles apparently performed by Columba which do not have such close Biblical precedents. These involve him interacting with the indigenous pagan belief system of the people whom he meets on his forays into the Scottish mainland, particularly the Picts. The stories of his encounters with what anthropologists would call 'primal religion' fall into two broad categories. The first group tells of the Saint baptizing a pagan shrine or symbol, usually by blessing it, with the result that it is 'converted' and Christianized. A good example of this is the episode recounted by Adomnan (Book 2, Chapter 11) where he blesses a well worshipped by the people despite the fact that all who drank or washed at it were struck down by 'the devil's art' and left half blind, crippled or leprous. As a result of Columba's blessing, the well loses its old malevolent power and develops healing properties. The second group of stories show Columba actually taking on and out-gunning pagan wizards and sorcerers by working a more potent and spectacular magic than they do. Adomnan gives a good example in Book 2, Chapter 34 of his *Life,* when he describes Columba dispersing a mist which the wizard Broichan had brought down to prevent him sailing up Loch Ness and then turning round a contrary wind conjured up by the wizard so that it is favourable and behind him. Adomnan also recounts a similar trial of strength taking place between the Saint and the pagan advisers of Brude in the Pictish king's stronghold (Book 2, Chapter 33) in a scene that is strongly reminiscent of the legendary encounter between St Patrick and Laogaire, the pagan high king of Ireland, on the sacred hill of Tara.

These stories point us to two important and in some ways contradictory aspects of the relationship between the new religion of Christianity and the old primal or pagan religion of the British Isles from the sixth century onwards. At one level, early Christian leaders like Columba seem to have sought to incorporate elements of the old faith by baptizing or converting them. This was perhaps particularly the case with practices such as the worship of wells and other sacred places which could be blessed and brought within the Christian economy of salvation without too much difficulty. Yet at the same time Columba and his Christian contemporaries also seem to have confronted and taken on pagan priests and magicians. This is the clear message of the encounter with Broichan. There is a sense here of an almost tit-for-tat contest between the representatives of paganism and Christianity with each side seeking to show that they can work the bigger and better miracles. It is notable that nearly all of these contests are depicted as taking place in front of pagan audiences and are located in Pictland. Adomnan concludes his account of Columba's quelling of the Loch Ness monster, which apparently only had to hear his voice to recoil in terror, with the observation that 'Even the heathen natives who were present at the time were so moved by the greatness of the miracle that they had witnessed that they too magnified the God of the Christians'.[3] In similar vein he reports King Brude changing his attitude to Columba when the Saint threw open the doors of the Pictish fortress which had been barred against him, apparently simply by making the sign of the Cross: 'From that day forward for as long as he lived, the ruler treated the holy and venerable man with great honour as was fitting'.[4]

As well as pointing to the ambivalent and complex nature of the relationship between Christianity and paganism, these miracle stories also raise the question of how far Columba's early followers and biographers sought to portray him not just as a Christian saint but also as a hero and strong man in the tradition of the Celtic warrior aristocracy. This is a much debated topic. In their recent collection of poems from Iona, Thomas Owen Clancy and Gilbert Markus show the extent to which the *'Amra Choluimb Chille'*, the eulogy commissioned very shortly after Columba's death by Aed mac Ainmirech, king of the Cenél Conaill, draws on the language used for pre-Christian Celtic heroes.[5] Other scholars are more cautious about seeing pre-Christian strands in the Irish cult of sainthood and feel that it marks a radical departure from the old tradition of celebrating the heroic lives of chieftains and warlords. Columba himself, of course, had both the old and the new types of heroism in his make-up. The blood of generations of warlords in his Cenél Connail ancestry mingled with the self-sacrificing asceticism and humility of one who followed Jesus of Nazareth. It would be surprising if his own sainthood, as it came to be asserted and celebrated by his disciples and successors, did not contain something of both these elements.

One aspect of Columba's supernatural power that can be seen either as wholly and exclusively Christian or alternatively as embracing substantial elements from primal Celtic mythology is his frequent encounter with angels and other non-physical beings. The pre-Christian Celts inhabited a world populated by spirits, fairies and demons which often took on physical shape and appeared to mortals. Second sight is a recognized feature of the Celtic character and one would expect Christianity in Celtic lands to take on a particular fascination with the supernatural and the otherworldly. Yet we need to be careful before putting down Adomnan's frequent references to Columba's sightings of both demons and angels to the survival of an essentially pre-Christian world picture. Early Christians also lived in constant contact with supernatural beings, as of course did the writers of the books that make up the Old and New Testaments. When Adomnan wrote of Columba seeing 'a line of foul black devils armed with iron spikes and drawn up ready for battle' or 'holy angels fighting in the air against the power of the Adversary' he was echoing the language of Revelation.[6] In seeing the souls of the righteous physically being carried by angels to heaven, the Saint himself was similarly sharing the same vision that had animated St Luke's account of the death of Lazarus.

Columba is not just portrayed by Adomnan and his other biographers as having visions of supernatural beings. He is also frequently described as being himself surrounded by angels or by heavenly light so that those looking at him see also a vision of another world. Typical of these 'close encounters of a supernatural kind' is the story related in Adomnan's *Life* (Book 3, Chapter 17) where St Brendan, attending mass in the church on the island of Hinba, 'saw a radiant ball of fire shining very brightly from St Columba's head as he stood in front of the altar and consecrated the sacred oblation. It shone upwards like a column of light and lasted until the mysteries were completed.'[7] Once again, this kind of picture is not without Biblical precedent and we are reminded how richly and vividly early Christians followed the writers of the Old and New Testaments in imagining their faith, rather than conceptualizing and rationalizing it, especially as later generations in the churches of the west have been inclined to do. Columba does not seem to have had any hint of the matter-of-fact reductionism and demand for rational explanation which characterize the modern post-Enlightenment outlook. Rather, whether out of Celtic feyness or Christian conviction, he seems to have had a decidedly mystical bent. Speaking to some of his brethren on Iona about his gift for prophecy, he revealed that 'by divine grace he had several times experienced a miraculous enlarging of the grasp of the mind so that he seemed to look at the whole world caught in one ray of sunlight'.[8]

If there was an ethereal mystical quality to Columba's saintliness, it also had a very earthy and human side. This is revealed in some of the subjects of his prophesying, which included the falling of a book into a water butt and the spilling of a horn of ink. It is also evident in his miracles. One of which I am particularly fond involves the Saint's powerful singing voice, which is attested to in a number of early sources. It is worth quoting Adomnan's story of what happened in full.

> The saint was saying vespers as usual with a few brethren, outside the king's fort, and some wizards came quite close to them, trying as best they could to make them stop. For they were afraid that the heathen people would hear the sound of God's praise from the brethren's mouths. Knowing this, St Columba began to chant the forty-fourth psalm, and at that moment his voice was miraculously lifted up in the air like some terrible thunder, so that the king and his people were filled with unbearable fear.[9]

Earlier Adomnan had commented that often when the Saint was chanting the psalms in church, people more than a mile away could make out every word of the verses he sang although to those standing with him in church his voice did not sound exceptionally loud. John Purser, the distinguished Scottish musicologist, has suggested that Columba may well have mastered the technique of emphasizing the harmonics that exist in everyone's voice so giving the impression that he had two voices, one sounding the harmonic an octave below the sung note and giving the impression of a lion-like growl that might well frighten those who had not heard it before, and the other sounding as though it emanated from somewhere far above the singer's head.[10] It may just be that Columba was an exceptionally loud and enthusiastic singer with a particular talent for vocal projection. Certainly, he often seems to have expressed his spirituality in song. One of the most vivid descriptions in Adomnan's life tells of how the Saint spent three days and nights fasting and praying in his small hut on Hinba: 'From the house rays of brilliant light could be seen at night, escaping through the chinks of the doors and through the keyholes. He was also heard singing spiritual chants of a kind never heard before'.[11]

These pictures of Columba chanting psalms, either in church with the brethren or alone in his retreat on Hinba, take us to the heart of his life as a monk. The daily office on Iona revolved around the singing of psalms just as it does in the late twentieth-century Benedictine Abbey at Pluscarden, near Elgin, where the monks still chant in Latin, as Columba did, and work their way through all 150 psalms every week. Columba's own deep attachment to the psalms is attested by numerous stories and sources. According to one tradition it was his childhood habit of visiting the little church of Tulach Dubhglaise, close to his birthplace, to read the psalms that led local children to nickname him *Colum Cille* (dove of the church). The Irish *Life* records that when his tutor, Cruithnechan, forgot the words of Psalm 100 while officiating at a Christmas mass the young Columba, who had only just learned to read, immediately stepped in and recited the psalm without a single mistake. Then there is the story that the offence for which he was punished at the Synod of Teltown and perhaps banished from Ireland was the illegal copying of a particularly fine psalter belonging to Finian of Moville. We know from Adomnan's *Life* and the early eulogistic poems that Columba spent many hours in his cell copying the psalms. We may even have one of the psalters he produced in the form of the *Cathach* preserved in the Royal Irish Academy in Dublin that bears his name. One of the oldest examples of Irish Latin script, this badly damaged and incomplete psalter, which follows the text of St Jerome's translation, has been reliably dated to either the late sixth or early seventh century so it is by no means impossible that it was the work of Columba himself. If it was, then the Saint was proficient in the art of manuscript illumination. The capital letters at the beginning of each psalm are decorated with spirals, stemmed crosses and the occasional fish or animal head. The *Cathach* is also notable for its use of the device of diminution whereby the initial letters get progressively smaller as they merge into the text.

The most powerful testimony to Columba's devotion to the psalms is to be found in the Irish *Life's* description of his nightly routine on Iona. Here the Saint is portrayed as sleeping for just a brief time on the bare earth floor of his cell with a stone pillar for his pillow. Rising, he first cried a lament, 'like a fond mother be-wailing her only son', and then went down to the seashore where he chanted all 150 psalms ('the three fifties') before sunrise each morning:

> *The three fifties, a heavy burden,*
> *throughout the night, great was the pain,*
> *in the sea alongside Scotland,*
> *before the sun would rise.*
> *Clearly he would lay himself*
> *in the sand — it was a heavy labour,*
> *the outline of his ribs through his garment*
> *was evident when the wind blew.*[12]

It is worth noting in passing that Columba is by no means the only Celtic saint who is said to have chanted the psalms by the sea. Bede describes St Cuthbert wading into the waves off Lindis-farne for the same purpose and adds that a pair of otters would sometimes greet him after his long vigil and lick his feet to warm them. One of the reasons why St David acquired the nickname *Aquaticus* is said to have been because he also was prone to stand up to his waist in the sea off Pembrokeshire and chant the psalms in time with the breaking waves.

This description of Columba's nightly vigil by the shore con-veys an impression of extreme asceticism and self-denial. More than any other source, the mid-twelfth-century Irish *Life* stresses the simplicity and humility of his monastic life. For example, it portrays him taking off the sandals of his fellow monks so that he could wash their feet and bringing their share of corn from the fields on his own back before grinding it himself in the island mill. It may well be that these stories have an element of hagiographical exaggeration yet it is hard to feel that there is not some foundation of fact behind them. There is also a ring of truth to the Irish *Life's* description of Columba's typical day on Iona: 'He observed the canonical hours, he offered the sacrifice of Christ's body and blood, he preached the gospel, baptized, consecrated and anointed. He healed lepers, the blind, the lame, and those with every other disease.'[13]

Monk, priest, preacher, pastor and healer — Columba seems to have fulfilled all of these roles as abbot of Iona. Central to his day was the performance of the monastic offices, celebrated together with other monks in the community's simple wooden church, and the times of private prayer undertaken alone in his cell on Iona and on the remote island of Hinba to which he seems often to have retreated for a period of solitary vigil and fasting. He regularly seems to have presided over celebrations of the Eucharist and to have preached both on Iona and during his travels on the mainland. Adomnan recounts several instances of his baptism of Christian converts and records healing miracles performed through prayer, the laying on of hands and sprinkling with water that he had blessed. He also provides telling examples of the Saint's deep pastoral skills, notably in the story of the wife who comes to him because she can no longer face sleeping with her ugly husband. She hopes that Columba will tell her to cross the sea and join a women's monastery but in fact he gets her and her husband to fast with him for a day. As they sleep the following evening, he prays for them and the next day the woman awakes transformed — 'The husband whom I hated I love today. My heart was changed from loathing to love'.[14]

Several stories speak in similar terms of Columba's abilities to reconcile people both to themselves and to others from whom they have become distant or estranged. This pastoral gift is often portrayed as being exercised through the medium of penance. Many of those who visited Iona came as penitents, seeking to atone for some crime or to come to terms with feelings of guilt and remorse. Columba seems to have established a special community for penitents at Mag Luinge on Tiree. A story told by Adomnan (Book 2, Chapter 39) shows the extent to which he used both penance and counselling as part of a pastoral ministry founded on the principles of reconciliation and justice. It concerns an Irishman who had killed a man in his native Connaught and had made the long journey to Iona to 'wipe out his sins on a pilgrimage'. Columba told him that he must spend seven years on Tiree. At the end of that period, he returned to the Saint to be told that he must now return to the relative who had paid his ransom and saved him from paying the penalty of death. He had promised this man he would serve him for life but had run away. Columba even gave him a decorated sword to give to the deserted master as a peace offering and told him to discharge his debt to his estranged family. This was done and the penitent returned to Iona, took his monastic vows and served for many years as a monk at Mag Luinge where he worked gathering reeds.

Columba was active as a teacher and scholar as well as a priest and pastor. On at least one occasion Adomnan refers to him with a pupil whom he is instructing in wisdom and divine learning (Book 3, Chapter 20). The monastic school at Iona was to become highly celebrated in the seventh century. I have already alluded to the frequency with which Columba is portrayed, as he is on the front cover of this book, copying the psalms at a desk in his cell. This work seems to have extended to other parts of the Scriptures, notably the Gospels, and may well have spread beyond simple copying of the text to Biblical scholarship and analysis. Adomnan comments on Columba's ability to interpret 'the sacred books' in the context of his more general prophetic powers (Book 3, Chapter 18) while Dallán Forgaill's 'Amra Choluimb Chille' mentions that he learned Greek grammar in order to aid his Biblical studies. This earliest of all the sources on his life in fact portrays Columba as 'learning's pillar in every stronghold' with intellectual interests stretching beyond Biblical exegesis and theology into the realms of mathematics and astronomy:

> He fixed the Psalms,
> he made known the books of Law,
> those books Cassian loved ...
> The books of Solomon, he followed them.
> Seasons and calculations he set in motion.
> He separated the elements according to figures
> among the books of the Law.
> He read mysteries
> and distributed the Scriptures among the schools,
> and he put together the harmony concerning
> the course of the moon,
> the course which it ran with the rayed sun,
> and the course of the sea.[15]

As the two most recent translators and editors of the *Amra* comment, it is interesting that 'this earliest specimen from Columba's dossier emphasizes not his miraculous powers ... but his learning. Dallán's Columba is above all a scholar's saint'.[16]

Did Columba write himself as well as studying the works of others? A host of poems have been attributed to him, many of them on very dubious grounds. There is, however, good reason for thinking that he did write devotional verses, some of which may have come down to us to provide a first-hand flavour of his mind and his faith. Various pieces of evidence suggest that Columba may have been a poet. There is the tradition that Gemmán, mentioned by Adomnan as Columba's teacher while he was a deacon at Leinster, was a bard who inspired his young charge with a love of the rich body of pre-Christian Irish verse. Adomnan also refers to a 'book of the week's hymns written out by St Columba with his own hand'.[17] Unfortunately it is not clear from this reference, which suggests that the Iona monks had their own weekly cycle of hymns in addition to the psalms, whether Columba was the book's author or simply its copier. However, a line in the *Amra* — 'He went with two songs to heaven after his cross' has generally been taken to refer to hymns written by the Saint although it could, I suppose, simply indicate that he pursued his love of singing to the very end of his life.[18]

The leading contenders for the Columban hymns mentioned in the *Amra,* if such they be, are probably two Latin poems which begin respectively *'Altus Prosator'* and *'Adiutor Laborantium'*. Two more poems, *'In Te, Christe'*, which has been freely translated to provide two modern hymns still found in a number of hymnals, and *'Noli Pater'*, also have long-standing traditions of attribution to Columba. It is worth considering the themes of these four poems in some detail and the circumstances apparently surrounding their composition.

Of the numerous poems that have been attributed to Columba over the years, scholars are generally agreed that *'Altus Prosator'* is the most likely to have been written by the Saint. James Kenney, who made an exhaustive survey of the sources for the early ecclesiastical history of Ireland, believes that we may 'with reasonable probability, regard the *Altus* as a genuine production of the saint of Iona'.[19] The poem has an 'abecedarian' shape with the first word of each verse beginning with a successive letter of the alphabet from A through to Z, although excluding J, U and W, making a total of 23 six-line stanzas. Strongly focused on the person of God the Father, it centres on the themes of creation, fall and judgement. It begins with a majestic evocation of the eternal nature of God and a clear exposition of the orthodox Christian theology of the Trinity:

> *The High Creator, Ancient of Days and Unbegotten*
> *was without origin of beginning and without end;*
> *He is and shall be to infinite ages of ages*
> *with Whom is Christ the only begotten*
> *and the Holy Spirit,*
> *coeternal in the everlasting glory of the Godhead.*
> *We set forth not three gods,*
> *but we say there is One God,*
> *saving our faith in three most glorious persons.*[20]

The hymn goes on to catalogue the physical wonders of creation in verses full of cosmological and astronomical imagery, perhaps reflecting Columba's strong interest in these themes as reported in the *Amra*:

> *By the divine powers of the great God is suspended*
> *the globe of earth, and thereto is set the circle*
> *of the great deep*
> *supported by the strong hand of God Almighty,*
> *promontories and rocks sustaining the same,*
> *with columns like bars on solid foundations*
> *immoveable like so many strengthened bases.*[21]

The fall of creation is then graphically described and one stanza is entirely given over to a lurid portrayal of hell. The hymn is pervaded by a sense of impending judgement — it has been compared to the later *'Dies Irae'* — and it portrays Christ not so much as the world's redeemer but rather as its judge, at whose descent from heaven 'the stars will fall to the earth as the fruit from a figtree'. The stress throughout the *'Altus Prosator'* is on the sovereignty and judgement of God. Its overall mood is dark and somewhat frightening. Indeed, with its concentration on the fall and on judgement it seems more Calvinist than Celtic, at least in the sense with which the latter term has been used in recent times.

The preface to the hymn which appears in the Irish *Liber Hymnorum* — an eleventh-century manuscript that cannot be taken as wholly reliable — gives two different versions of how Columba came to compose it. One is that it was written as a penitential exercise by the Saint who was troubled by the memory of three battles in which he had played a part, Cúl Drebene in 561, Coleraine in 579 and Cúl Feda near Clonard in 587. The other tradition recorded in the *Liber Hymnorum* and in several other early manuscripts has it that the words of *'Altus Prosator'* came to Columba as he was grinding oats at the mill on Iona in order to make bread for visitors to the monastery. The particular rhythm of the poem, with eight syllables to each line, is said to have been suggested to him by the motion of the quern, or rotary hand mill, that he was using. For his 1992 BBC radio series, 'Scotland's Music', John Purser very successfully fitted *'Altus Prosator'* to an ancient quern tune which has an octosyllabic structure and a chant-like melody 'in character as dark as the original hymn'.[20]

The preface to *'Altus Prosatur'* in some manuscripts of the *Liber Hymnorum* gives the additional information that the visitors for whom Columba was making oat-bread were emissaries from Gregory the Great, Pope from 590 to 604, who had come to Iona bearing presents of a Cross and a hymnary. In return Columba gave them his newly written hymn to take back to Rome. It was duly read out to Pope Gregory who expressed his view that there was no fault with it 'except the scantiness in it of the praise of the Trinity'.[21] This criticism reached the ears of Columba who responded by writing another hymn, *'In Te, Christe'*, with a more Trinitarian and Christological focus. This story has been twisted to suggest that Gregory's initial complaint was that the *'Altus Prosator'* was too 'creation centred' and did not dwell enough on the theme of redemption. Unfortunately, however, the evidence from the *Liber Hymnorum*, which itself can hardly be taken as gospel, does not bear this interpretation. Nor does it really do justice to the theme of the *'Altus Prosator'* which, as we have seen, is centred as much on judgement as on creation although it does certainly lack a strong sense of the redemptive power of Christ.

Whatever its provenance, *'In Te, Christe'*, has become the best known to modern Christians of all the poems supposedly written by Columba. Translated by Duncan MacGregor at the end of the nineteenth century, it has supplied two hymns which are found in several modern hymnbooks, 'O God, thou art the father of all that have believed' and 'Christ is the world's redeemer, the lover of the pure'. The first of these is a fairly close translation of the first half of the original poem, while the second, generally sung to the ancient Irish tune 'Moville', follows the second half, which according to some manuscripts of the *Liber Hymnorum* is the only part actually composed by Columba. They can be found as numbers 397 and 301 in the current edition of the *Church Hymnary*, 52 and 219 in the Methodist book *Hymns and Psalms* and 73 and 272 in the United Reformed Church's *Rejoice and Praise*. The other hymn which is regularly attributed to Columba in modern hymnbooks, 'Alone with none but thee, my God' is certainly of early Irish origin but much less likely to have been written by the Saint of Iona.

A more likely Columban composition is the short hymn *'Adiutor Laborantium'*. Interestingly, it has close affinities with both the poems discussed so far, sharing with *'Altus Prosator'* an abecederian structure and echoing in its first line a phrase in the third line of *'In Te, Christe'* (*Deus in auditorium intende laborantium*). Only relatively recently discovered in an eleventh-century manuscript of devotional and liturgical material from Winchester, it is mentioned in the *Liber Hymnorum*, which curiously does not include it, as having been composed just before the *'Altus Prosator'* when Columba was walking from the refectory to the mill on Iona with the sack of oats on his back. This may explain the first line of what is in effect a litany of God's attributes, 'O helper of workers'. The hymn dramatically changes mood half way through and becomes a much more personal cry for help:

> *I beg that me, a little man*
> *trembling and most wretched,*
> *rowing through the infinite storm*
> *of this age,*
> *Christ may draw after Him to the lofty*
> *most beautiful haven of life ...*[24]

This graphic metaphor of the individual human soul 'rowing through the infinite storm' surely comes from the pen, if not of Columba himself, then of one of his fellow brothers on Iona. Facing regular journeys across the sea surrounding their island base with its treacherous currents and whirlpools, they must have been all too aware of the fragility and vulnerability of human life. Adomnan recounts several instances of storms suddenly blowing up, and the Irish Annals record the wrecking of several boats carrying members of the community to and from Iona with serious loss of life. In 691, for example, six monks are reported to have drowned when their boat was overturned in a severe gale.

The fourth poem attributed to Columba in early Irish manuscript sources is also a cry for God's protection against disaster. 'Noli Pater' begins with a plea to God not to allow thunder and lightning 'lest we be shattered by its fear and its fire'. One of the manuscripts of the *Liber Hymnorum* suggests that Columba composed it when an oakwood had been set alight by a bolt of lightning. Another version, which also mentions lightning setting fire to a wood, relates that he offered up the short hymn, which continues by expressing both fear and praise of God, while standing at the door of a hermitage in Derry. Its association with an oakwood carries echoes of pre-Christian Celtic religion where oak groves were particularly sacred and the location for the sacrificial rituals carried out by Druids, and there is something of the feel of a charm or incantation about the hymn. According to the preface in the *Liber Hymnorum*, 'whoever recites it at lying down and rising up, it protects him against lightning flash, and it protects the nine persons of his household whom he chooses.'[25] A more Christian gloss on the poem in another manuscript suggests that it is, in fact, an allegory on the theme of the Last Judgement. Whatever its purpose and provenance, it ends with a delightful and wholly Christian image:

*The flame of God's love dwells in my heart
as a jewel of gold is placed in a silver dish.*[26]

The themes of praise, protection, presence and penitence which sound through these four poems were all, as we shall see, central concerns of Columban Christianity. Whether they represent the work of Columba himself, or the work of those who followed him, it is impossible to know. What we can say, however, is that they are very much more likely to have been penned by the Saint than the many other more romantic verses which are often attributed to him. The poems which portray Columba looking back longingly to Ireland or scanning the sea in the hope of seeing one of the great sea monsters (presumably whales) that he considered the most wondrous creatures of the deep are almost certainly of much later origin. There is one other poem traditionally attributed to him, however, that I cannot resist quoting here even though it was almost certainly written by another. I do so not to provide relief and escape from the rather dark and sombre tone of much of his own work, if indeed it is represented by the four hymns we have been considering above, but rather because I think it beautifully expresses the wonderful variety of his activities on Iona and captures that quality of the rhythm of life which I have already suggested was central to the Irish monastic tradition and of which he was so striking an exemplar.

> *That I might bless the Lord*
> *Who orders all;*
> *Heaven with its countless bright orders,*
> *Land, strand and flood,*
> *That I might search in all the books*
> *That would help my soul;*
> *At times kneeling to the Heaven of my heart,*
> *At times singing psalms;*
> *At times contemplating the King of Heaven,*
> *Chief of the Holy Ones;*
> *At times at work without compulsion,*
> *This would be delightful.*
> *At times plucking duilisc from the rocks*
> *At other times fishing*
> *At times distributing food to the poor*
> *At times in a hermitage.*[27]

The diverse activities so beautifully intertwined in that poem, priestly, pastoral, scholarly and manual, are brought together in Adomnan's extraordinarily moving account of the Saint's last days on Iona. It is difficult to do justice to this passage without reproducing it in full and those readers who do not know it are urged to have recourse to one of the excellent modern translations of Adomnan's life and savour it for themselves. Suffice it to say that in his last hours on earth Columba is portrayed as engaging in many of the activities that have characterized his lifelong ministry. He goes round the island in a cart visiting the brothers at work in the fields and telling them of his forthcoming death. He attends Sunday mass and has a vision of 'an angel of the Lord flying above actually inside the house of prayer'. He blesses the heaps of grain stored in the barn ready for the community's use through the winter. Then, after his poignant encounter with the old horse which used to carry the milk-pails and which now puts its head against his bosom and weeps, he climbs the little hill overlooking the monastery and blesses the island, prophesying that it will come to be reverenced by Christians and non-Christians far round the world. Returning to his hut, he sits copying out the psalms, stopping when he reaches the tenth verse of Psalm 34: 'Those that seek the Lord shall not want for anything that is good'. He then goes to vespers and returns to sleep on the bare rock floor of his hut with a stone for his pillow. After briefly resting, he summons the brethren, telling them to 'love one another unfeignedly' and commending them to God's infinite mercy. As the bell rings out for the midnight office, he runs ahead of them into church and kneels in prayer before the altar. At that moment the whole church is filled with angelic light around the Saint. Helped by his faithful servant Diarmait, he raises his right arm to bless the choir of monks and at that moment the venerable abbot gives up the ghost, his face transfixed with a wonderful joy and gladness 'for he could see the angels coming to meet him'.[28]

Columba's passing from the world, like his arrival into it, was accompanied by signs and wonders, miracles and angelic apparitions. In death his powers of prophecy, pastoral aid and protection were to be undiminished. Indeed, his stature as a saint grew steadily as the cult of Columba spread far beyond the bounds of the tiny island on which he had chosen to spend the last thirty five years of his life.

Notes

1   George Campbell, 8th Duke of Argyll, *Iona* (Strahan & Co., London, 1870), pp. 42 & 43
2   Thomas Owen Clancy and Gilbert Markus, *IONA*, p.116
3   Adomnan of Iona, *Life of Columba*, p. 176
4   *Ibid.*, p.184
5   Thomas Owen Clancy and Gilbert Markus, *op.cit.*, pp.123-24
6   Adomnan of Iona, *op.cit.*, pp. 211, 210. Compare Revelation 12.7
7   *Ibid.*, p.219
8   *Ibid.*, p.112
9   *Ibid.*, p.141
10   John Purser, *Scotland's Music* (Mainstream Publishing, Edinburgh 1992), p.33-34

11   Adomnan of Iona, *op.cit.*, p. 220
12   Maíri Herbert, *op.cit.*, p. 264
13   *Ibid.*, p.264
14   Adomnan of Iona, *op.cit.*, p. 195
15   Thomas Owen Clancy and Gilbert Markus, *op.cit.*, pp. 107-9
16   *Ibid.*, p.122
17   Adomnan of Iona, *op. cit.*, p. 160
18   Thomas Owen Clancy and Gilbert Markus, *op. cit.*, p. 111
19   James Kenney, *The Sources for the Early History of Ireland: Ecclesiastical* (Pádraic ó Táilliúr, Dublin, 1979), p.263
20   *The Irish Liber Hymnorum* edited by J.H. Bernard and R. Atkinson (Henry Bradshaw Society, London, 1898), vol.II, p.150
21   *Ibid.*, p.152
22   John Purser, *op.cit.*, p.34
23   *Liber Hymnorum*, vol.II, p.25
24   Thomas Owen Clancy and Gilbert Markus, *op.cit.*, p.73
25   *Liber Hymnorum*, vol.II, p.28
26   Thomas Owen Clancy and Gilbert Markus, *op.cit.*, p.85
27   *The Poem Book of the Gael* edited and translated by Eleanor Hull (Chatto and Windus, London, 1912), p.237
28   Adomnan of Iona, *op. cit.*, p.229

4

The character of the Columban Church

Did Columba introduce or exemplify a new and distinctive form of Christian doctrine and practice? Can we, indeed, speak of Columban Christianity in the same way that we can talk about Lutheranism, Methodism or Benedictine monasticism?

To begin to answer these questions we need to strip away more layers of myth-making. Over the 1400 years since his death Columba has been hailed by apologists from many different denominational and theological standpoints as the precursor or founding father of their particular brand of faith. Scottish Presbyterians, Episcopalians and Roman Catholics have perhaps been the most assiduous claimants to the Columban heritage, each maintaining that the church which he planted on Iona anticipated in some important respect their own distinctive denominational characteristics. This anachronistic and partisan use of history was roundly and rightly condemned more than a century ago by the eighth Duke of Argyll. Noting that the distinctive features of the monastic system introduced by Columba on Iona 'have much exercised the ingenuity of Presbyterian and Episcopalian controversialists', he pointed to the futility of looking 'in the peculiarities of the Scoto-Irish Church for the model either of primitive practice or of any modern system. As regards the theology of Columba's time, although it was not what we now understand as Roman, neither assuredly was it what we understand as Protestant.'[1]

The fact is that, unlike Martin Luther, John Calvin or John Wesley, Columba was not the instigator of a new movement in the history of Christianity nor the founder of a new church. Indeed, he himself would have had no sense of belonging to a distinct denomination as most Christians do today. He belonged to an age where the church was thought of in universal terms rather than as a series of national or confessional bodies. Columba owed his allegiance first and foremost to Jesus Christ. He had a strong sense of the universality of the family which made up the members of His body on earth. This is not to say that he did not have other more particular and personal loyalties as well. As we have already seen, he retained strong ties of kinship with the Uí Néill princes in northern Ireland. He doubtless thought of himself as Irish and identified with fellow Irish settlers (*Scoti*) in Dál Riata. This particular sense of ethnic and cultural identity may have been intensified by the difficulty in communicating with other peoples in what is now Scotland, most notably the Picts since he needed an interpreter when preaching to them. Writing recently about the monks of Iona, including Columba, Donald Meek, Professor of Celtic at the University of Aberdeen, has sensibly if tentatively suggested that 'they might have regarded themselves as Irish or Gaelic, if indeed they had any rudimentary notion of these matters. More probably, they would have defined themselves over and against the Picts and the Britons with whom they came into contact'.[2]

Columba would most certainly not have seen himself belonging to the kind of distinct Celtic Church so often associated with him by historians and Christians of a romantic persuasion. The notion of a Celtic Church, conceived of as a distinct ecclesiastical entity clearly distinguishable from, if not actually in opposition to the Roman Church, is profoundly misleading. It presupposes a degree of uniformity among the highly diverse Celtic tribes and peoples of Europe and a sense of self-conscious separatism which simply did not exist. The modern revival of interest in so-called 'Celtic Christianity' has unfortunately perpetuated and encouraged the myth of the Celtic Church. We need to heed the sober and salutary words of Professor Wendy Davies of University College, London: 'There was no such thing as a Celtic Church: the concept is unhelpful, if not positively harmful'.[3]

This does not mean that there was nothing to distinguish the Christian beliefs and practices of the Irish-born and educated Columba from those of his near-contemporary Augustine of Canterbury, whose theological education and monastic experience had been in Rome. The invention by over-zealous Protestants and nationalists of a wholly spurious Celtic Church standing over and against the Roman Church has had more than one distorting effect. As well as greatly over-exaggerating the extent of distinct and self-conscious Celtic separatism, it has also provoked a counter-reaction which has equally over-stated the Roman influence on all early medieval Christian communities, including those in the British Isles. An example of this is Professor Jocelyn Toynbee's statement that 'the so-called Celtic Church, surviving continuously in the west and north, was thoroughly Roman in Creed and origins; Roman too, initially in its organization and practice'.[4] It is true that the theology of Columba, based as it was on the Scriptures, the writings of the Latin and Greek Fathers and the historic creeds of the church, would have struck Augustine as essentially orthodox and that he would have found much that was familiar in the Latin liturgy used on Iona with its close affinity to the Roman ordinary of the Mass. In other areas, however, there were striking differences between both the outlook and the practices prevailing in Canterbury and Iona most notably in ecclesiastical organisation, monastic lifestyle and spirituality and devotion.

The numerous Christian communities which were in existence throughout Europe, North Africa and the Eastern Mediterranean by the sixth century AD exhibited a rich diversity of local cultural, social, intellectual and liturgical influences and practices. The Christian church may have been conceived of in much more universal, international and non-denominational terms than it is now but it was not monolithic in its structures and ethos. Geographical and linguistic factors undoubtedly played a part in bringing certain communities together and forging particular spheres of common influence and practice. These were not always as one might expect — Iona, in common with other monastic communities on the western side of the British Isles, had at least as much contact with Egyptian and Syrian Christianity as with Rome. There were also elements of xenophobic chauvinism at work as well. A seventh-century Irish abbot was said to have held that 'Rome is wrong. Jerusalem is wrong. Antioch is wrong. Only the *Scoti* and Britons know what is right'. Given their close geographical proximity, it was not surprising that Christian communities formed by the Irish, the British and the Picts should display certain affinities as well as have their own distinct local characteristics. Increasingly anthropologists and historians of religion stress the theme of inculturation, the extent to which all faiths, including Christianity, adapt themselves to and are shaped by the particular cultures in which they take root. As Thomas Owen Clancy and Gilbert Markus point out, to dismiss such phrases as Celtic Christianity and the Celtic Church is not to rule out any connection between the local cultures of the Celtic peoples and the way they practised Christianity. 'It is only to deny that it was the same "Celtic" way among all these peoples. Christianity had its local, particular aspects in early Ireland and Britain, but its aspects were many and varied from region to region and from people to people.'[5]

Essentially this chapter, and indeed this book as a whole, is dealing with one of these particular strands, or 'inculturations' of Christianity in Celtic Britain. We are, I think, justified in calling it Columban Christianity or perhaps even more accurately the Columban Church. Columba, as we have already seen, was a church planter. If he did not found a new denomination or a new movement, he manifestly *did* found monasteries, most notably on Iona and also elsewhere in Scots Dál Riata and in Ireland. These monasteries formed a definite *paruchia* or family, which came to have their own common rule at least in the century following Columba's death if not during his lifetime. The Columban *familia*, which grew considerably in both size and importance through the seventh and eighth centuries, looked for leadership to successive abbots of Iona in the highly personalized form of authority and organization which had been established by the founder. Sally Foster has rightly observed that 'the term "Columban Church" is not without drawbacks since it plays down the unsung role of less well-documented saints'[6] but it is infinitely preferable to 'the Celtic Church' and provided we use it carefully to describe the particular characteristics of the Christian community which flourished on Iona and its wider *paruchia* from the mid-sixth to the mid-ninth centuries, it can, I think, be positively helpful and fruitful.

The single most striking and important feature of the Columban Church was its monastic character. In this, of course, it corresponded to earlier Irish foundations associated with such figures as Finnian of Clonard, Finnian of Moville and Ciarán of Clonmacnoise, although not with the church established by St Patrick in the mid-fifth century. The extent to which Patrick deliberately sought to provide Ireland with an episcopally administered church organized on a diocesan system with parish churches as the key units of local mission is a matter of some debate. What is not in dispute is that within a generation or so of his death the dominant institution of Irish Christianity had become the monastery, with the parish church being eclipsed in importance and the authority of diocesan bishops having been effectively taken over by abbots. Columba was, of course, the supreme exemplar of an abbot who wielded far more power and influence than a bishop, a matter which Bede found particularly worthy of note. However he always seems to have deferred to the authority of a visiting bishop in liturgical matters and allowed him to celebrate the Eucharist.

The apparent subordination of bishops to abbots in the Columban Church has long been made much of by Presbyterians and others seeking historical precedents for non-episcopal forms of ecclesiastical government. In fact, it is unlikely to have rested on any high-minded theories of democracy or power-sharing based on Biblical principles. Monasteries took root in Ireland because they suited the social and geographical configuration of the country. Parish churches and dioceses worked well in more centralized and urbanized societies but were not appropriate for remote rural communities. The structure of the monastic *familia* paralleled that of the *túaths*, the small kingships into which Ireland was divided. It was not surprising that in a society based on ties of kinship and family, abbots should come to take on something of the status of kings, especially since many, like those of Iona, held their office through hereditary succession. Monastic *paruchiae* formed tribes which coexisted alongside their secular equivalents. As well as becoming the spiritual centres of the *túaths*, monasteries adopted some of the physical characteristics of the hill-forts and strongholds of their rulers, being protected by a *vallum*, or boundary bank and ditch, and a wooden stockade which surrounded a small township of dwelling huts, workshops and communal buildings.

It was this Irish model of being the church that Columba brought to Scotland when he planted his community on Iona in or around 563. In the words of the Scottish historian Archie Duncan, 'What Columba brought was not a Gospel hitherto unheard, but a way of religious life in eremitical communities following the rule of the founder abbot and seeking spiritual maturity through work and meditation'.[7] Behind its immediate Irish antecedents lay deeper roots which gave the monastic life of Iona and of the Columban church as a whole much of its special character. The origins of Christian monasticism lie in fourth-century Egypt and Syria where the desert fathers felt the call to withdraw from the world and either retreat into solitary cells or establish corporate communities living according to a strict rule of life. The pioneer of the eremitical or solitary life is often taken to be St Antony of Egypt while the development of cenobitic or common-life monasticism is particularly associated with Pachomius. Introduced to western Europe through the writings of Athanasius and John Cassian, and the example of Martin of Tours who founded his own monastery at Ligugé in Gaul in 361, the ideas and practices of the desert fathers profoundly influenced Columba and his successors. References in early poems written by monks associated with Iona suggest that Athanasius' *Life of St Antony*, Sulpicius Severus' *Life of Martin of Tours* and Cassian's *Conferences*, which give an account of the teaching and practices of the early Egyptian monks and hermits, were among the most thumbed volumes in the island's library.

Several pieces of evidence point to trading contact between the eastern Mediterranean and Iona. Archaeological digs on the island have uncovered pieces of red pottery from Carthage in North Africa and fragments of *amphorae*, containers for olive oil and wine, thought to come from Asia Minor. Some of the pigments used for colouring illuminated manuscripts can only have been imported from the Near East and the little red dots which fringe the capital letters on the psalter traditionally associated with Columba and known as his *Cathach* seem to be inspired by decorative work found on Coptic manuscripts in Egyptian monasteries. It has even been suggested that the rectangular layout of the monastic settlement on Iona was based on an Egyptian or Syrian design. While one or two other Irish foundations were surrounded by a similar rectangular *vallum*, most notably Clonmacnoise, the great majority of both Irish and Scottish monastic compounds were circular in shape.

It is impossible to gain any impression of the scale or the appearance of the original monastery on Iona from the restored buildings of the much later Benedictine foundation which form the present abbey. Columba's community had no stone buildings and lived, worked, prayed and slept in a collection of wooden huts and wattle and daub shelters which covered an area possibly extending to twenty acres. Some monks lived alone while others seem to have enjoyed a more communal existence, sleeping in dormitories. At the centre of the compound was a small wooden church and around it the guest house, kitchen/refectory, library/scriptorium (where manuscripts were copied and studied), barns for storing grain, and the smithy and workshops for working with metal, wood, leather and glass. Scattered among these buildings stood high standing crosses, initially of wood and later of stone, commemorating important events in the history of the monastery or the life of the founder. Beyond the *vallum* were almost five hundred acres of fields on which the community kept cattle and sheep, and grew wheat, oats and other crops. A small fleet of boats was maintained both for fishing and for ferrying monks and visitors to and from the island.

It has been estimated that there may have been around one hundred and fifty monks resident on Iona by the time of Columba's death. They were divided into three main groupings — *seniores*, who were largely responsible for the services in church; working brothers, who seem to have done the bulk of the manual labour in the workshops and fields; and *juniores*, who were novices under instruction. It is not entirely clear if the distinction was made purely in terms of age or if there was a separate category of lay brothers who carried out much of the manual work. In addition to the resident novices, students and pupils came to the island for shorter periods of study. There was also a steady stream of guests and pilgrims passing through Iona, including monks from other communities and penitents seeking to atone for crimes and misdemeanours. Many were directed on to the remoter communities on Hinba and Tiree where monks from Iona also regularly went on solitary retreat to find their 'place of resurrection'. The general impression is of a busy and bustling community with a very cosmopolitan flavour. Although the original monks on Iona were probably all Irish, they were soon joined by recruits from other parts of the British Isles and possibly from further afield. The first of the community to die was a Briton and Adomnan mentions two Englishmen and a Pict among those monks on the island in Columba's time. Despite its remote location, and the fact that it could be cut off by bad weather for several days at a time, Iona was not isolated from the outside world. Pointing to the comprehensiveness of its library, Clancy and Markus comment: 'Here we find a monastery not out on a limb, doing its own "Celtic" thing, but steeped in the culture of Latin Christianity' — and, one might add, Eastern Christianity as well.[8]

It would be wrong to gain an impression of Iona as being primarily a transit camp-cum-tourist resort. It is true that there was much coming and going and this was why Columba put so much stress on hospitality and told his monks to minister to all their guests, including, as Adomnan's lovely story tells us, the crane which flew in from Ireland. It was the resident community of monks who constituted the heart and soul of the monastery, their lives of self-mortification and daily offering of the sacrifice of praise which provided its *raison d'être*. In common with the inmates of most Irish monasteries, the monks of Iona followed a lifestyle that was a good deal more strict and austere than that pursued by those in the Continental houses founded by St Benedict and his followers. Indeed, the influence on Irish monasticism of the radical asceticism of the desert fathers of Egypt and Syria provides one indisputable difference between Celtic and Roman Christianity in the early medieval period.

In his classic work on the subject written in 1931, John Ryan listed four main characteristics which made Irish monasticism distinctive. The first was its severe bodily austerity, exemplified in long periods of fasting and vigil, which he saw as deriving directly from Egypt. The leading figures in the monastic movement in Continental Europe, by contrast, took a much more relaxed view and prescribed a much less demanding lifestyle in their foundations. The daily rations which each monk was allowed by St Benedict, for example, included a pound of bread, two dishes of cooked food, a dish of fruit or young vegetables and more than half a pint of wine, a menu which, in Ryan's words, 'would have shocked the Fathers of the desert and have sounded incredible to Irish ears'.[9] Benedictine monks were also able to enjoy eight hours of unbroken sleep, a luxury denied to members of the Iona community who were awoken three times during the night for vigils.

The second distinctive feature of Irish monasticism singled out by John Ryan was the combination of eremitical and cenobitic practices within the same communities, with solitary anchorites and married monks living apparently quite happily alongside one another — a testimony, perhaps, to that balanced rhythm of life which we have already noted as a major theme in the Irish monastic tradition. Thirdly, he also pointed to a zeal for studying native language and literature as well as Biblical and theological literature in Latin and Greek and lastly he noted the prominence of abbots as ecclesiastical rulers, a development which he felt might partly have arisen 'from an ascetical fear of the worldly advantages then commonly attached to the episcopal office'. Abbots were entrusted with authority because they were felt to be less prone than bishops to worldly temptations and luxurious lifestyles.[10]

All four of these features are to be found in the Columban monastic *familia*. They also figure prominently in the monastic rule which bears the Saint's name. First found in Irish in a manuscript in the Burgundian Library in Brussels, *The Rule of Columcille* cannot be traced back beyond the ninth century and it is unlikely that it was actually the work of Columba himself. However, it is reasonable to assume that it embodies principles which had come to be established by his successors as abbots of Iona and it may well reflect the feelings of the founder. The rule, which is striking in its severity and austerity, begins with a commendation of both the eremitic and the cenobitic life and an injunction to 'be always naked in imitation of Christ'. This is followed by a call to develop 'a mind prepared for red martyrdom' (i.e. laying down one's life for the faith) and 'a mind fortified and steadfast for white martyrdom' (the form of witness to Christ particularly dear to the Irish saints which involved dying to self and to all attachments, leaving home and family and going into perpetual exile). Although not as specific as some Irish monastic rules which laid down detailed regulations concerning daily genuflections, vigils and periods of fasting and prayer, the one followed on Iona clearly stipulates a regime of rigorous self-denial:

> *Take not of food till thou art hungry.*
> *Sleep not till thou feelest desire.*
> *Speak not except on business.*[11]

The Rule of Columcille prescribes three daily labours: reading, work and prayer. The stress on reading reinforces what we have already observed in looking at Columba's own life about the importance of study and scholarship in the community on Iona. Manual work was also regarded as a staple ingredient of the monastic life. The rule divides it into three parts: 'thine own work, and the work of thy place as regards its real wants; secondly, thy share of the brethren's work; and lastly, to help thy neighbours, viz. by instruction, or writing, or sewing garments or whatever they may be in want of'.[12] The implication here seems to be that all members of the community took part in manual labour, not just the 'working brothers' whose special vocation it was. The third daily work, that of prayer and devotion, occupies the largest part of the rule. The monks are enjoined to 'constant prayers for those who trouble thee. Fervour in singing the office of the dead, as if every faithful dead was a particular friend of thine ... Let thy vigils be constant from eve to eve ... Thy measure of prayer shall be until thy tears come; or thy measure of work of labour till thy tears come; or thy measure of thy work of labour or of thy genuflections until thy perspiration often comes, if thy tears are not free'.[13]

What are we to make of this exhortation to tears, not as one might imagine of compassion, but rather of exhaustion? It brings us up against the hard and almost unbearably demanding ethos of Irish monasticism, a world away from the comfortable, easy, attractive spirituality of Celtic Christianity as it is often portrayed today. The constant injunctions to fasting and mortification, genuflection and self-flagellation that fill the gloomy penitentials and stern rules which come out of the early Irish monasteries and their offshoots on mainland Britain may seem unattractively and even dangerously masochistic to us today. That is because we have lost the sense which our ancestors had of the mysterious power of sacrifice, understood in terms of a reciprocal process of self-offering by God and self-giving by his creatures. Those who see Celtic Christianity as a 'user-friendly' self-oriented faith akin to the contemporary New Age movement could hardly be more wide of the mark. Columba and his contemporaries, so close in outlook to and so influenced by the demanding spirituality of the desert fathers, had a deep understanding and appreciation of the intimate if paradoxical connection between self-sacrifice and self-fulfilment, martyrdom and resurrection. We can only begin to enter into their minds as we engage with this dark and somewhat forbidding aspect of their faith.[14]

How then can we best discern and describe the distinctive essence of Columban Christianity, the faith and practice both of the Saint himself and of the church which he established on Iona and elsewhere? At the risk of gross over-simplification, and of sounding very sermonic, I propose answering this question by identifying a triple trio of themes. I employ this device partly because the number three was so important to the Celts, whose pre-Christian religion centred around triads of deities and whose Christianity found one of its most characteristic expressions in a particular devotion to the doctrine of the Trinity. For the remainder of this chapter I wish to explore the distinctive characteristics of the Columban Church in terms of a devotional base built on prayer, psalms and poetry, a theology of praise, protection and presence, and an ecclesiology (not a word that Columba and his followers would ever have dreamed of using) of penitence, provisionality and pilgrimage.

Prayer, undertaken both individually and corporately, was at the heart of the spiritual life of the Columban Church. The monks spent long periods praying alone in their cells, often standing with their arms outstretched and raised in what was known as the cross vigil. Several times during the day and night the ringing of a bell summoned them to church to recite the Divine Office. There seem to have been five canonical hours during the day — *prime, terce, sext, nones* and *vespers* — while the night office was apparently divided into three separate services —*Ad initium noctis* (at nightfall), *Ad medium noctis* (at midnight) and *Ad matutinam* (very early in the morning towards daybreak). Mass was celebrated on Sundays and feastdays at *sext*, the midday service.

We know relatively little about the forms of service used in the Columban Church. The main weekly celebration of the Eucharist on Iona seems to have taken place in the small church. The Gospel was read outside where lay members, catechumens (those undergoing instruction prior to baptism), penitents and visitors remained while the monks processed into the church with the presiding priest. Other services may well have taken place out of doors at the foot of the high standing crosses. There are references to services being sung and, as we have already noted, Adomnan mentions a book of weekly hymns which had either been copied out or written by Columba himself. It may well have resembled the *Bangor Antiphonary* which dates from the late seventh century and provides hymns for the Mass and other services. Unfortunately there are no surviving liturgies from Iona. The earliest Irish and Scottish liturgies which are still in existence — the *Stowe Missal* and the *Book of Deer*, both of which probably date from the early ninth century — broadly follow the Roman rite but also show traces of Gallican, Mozarabic (Spanish) and Eastern Mediterranean influence.

If it is impossible to reconstruct the eucharistic liturgy used on Iona during and after Columba's time, we are on much surer ground when it comes to the daily services held at the canonical hours. The Divine Office consisted primarily of the recitation of psalms. It is not quite clear how long it took the monks to get through all one hundred and fifty psalms though there is evidence that in Irish monasteries generally more psalms were chanted at each service, particularly during night vigils, than in either Continental European or Eastern monasteries. Columba's followers and successors seem to have shared his own special attachment to this part of the Scriptures. Chanted, recited, copied, studied and prayed, the psalms were central to the spiritual and devotional life of the Columban Church. Their imagery almost certainly influenced its theology. Certainly the three theological themes that I have identified as particularly strong in Columban Christianity — praise, protection and presence — are all very strongly represented in the psalter.

The psalms may well also have been a major influence on the third strand which I have identified in the devotional life of the Columban Church — its poetic quality. What I have in mind here is the tendency, shared by many other Celtic Christian communities, to pray in poems rather than in prose and to express faith in images rather than concepts. This is something that I have written about at much greater length in my book *The Celtic Way*.[15] It is not surprising that those so steeped in the vivid imagery of the psalms should be inclined to express their faith in this way and also to give more prominence in worship to the physical elements and to raw human emotions like anger and despair than other Christian traditions which have put more premium on reasonable moderation and carefully measured prose.

Other factors also contributed to this characteristic of the early British and Irish church. Pre-Christian Celtic society accorded a high role to poets. In Ireland, especially the *filid*, or bards, were a much venerated and respected group who were seen as guardians of the great oral tradition of folklore and heroic legend which sustained the community and provided its roots. Often attached to royal households, the *filid* effectively constituted a distinct order living off public subsidy. The coming of Christianity did not overthrow this reverence for poets and poetry although it brought about an important change in replacing an oral culture with a written one. The monks who toiled away in the monastic *scriptoria* did not simply copy psalters and Gospel books. They also wrote down, for the first time, poems and legends about heroes and battles from the pre-Christian past which had previously been passed down by word of mouth. Zeal for native language and literature was one of the characteristics which John Ryan noted as distinguishing Irish from Continental monasticism. It suggested a broad and inclusive approach affirming traditional poems and songs and integrating them in the new literary-based Christian culture.

There is a very interesting story which shows Columba defending poets at the convention of Druim Ceat in 575. Apparently some of those present sought to banish the bards because of 'the multitude and the sharpness of their tongues and their complaining and for their evil words. Moreover they had made satires against Aed, King of Ireland.'[16] Columba strongly opposed this proposal and argued instead that the order of *filid* should be reorganized and their number and privileges curtailed, a solution which seems to have been accepted. This portrayal of the Saint as a friend of the creative arts seems to square with what we know of the activities undertaken by the monks on Iona which appear to have included manuscript illumination, metalwork, leatherwork and jewellery making. Columba and his successors clearly valued creative imagination and felt that the arts stood not at the margins of the church but rather at its very centre.

Behind this encouragement of artists and poets lay a belief that story, symbol and metaphor were at least as important in putting across the mysteries of the Christian faith as argument, concept and debate. The Columban Church did not produce any great practitioners or texts in the disciplines of philosophical or systematic theology. This is not to say that there was no interest in the big questions with which they deal. Its theology, however, was rooted in its liturgy and devotional life and expressed in hymns of praise like *'Altus Prosator'* rather than being confined to the schoolroom or the study and formulated in academic treatises. The Columban Church, indeed, exemplified the principle of *lex orandi, lex credendi* — it was a worshipping community which believed that God was to be found through prayer and contemplation rather than a debating society which sought to find proofs and arguments for His existence through rigorous debate and disputation.

Having said that, is it possible to discern a distinctive Columban theology? It has been fashionable to suggest that Celtic Christianity as a whole developed a theology which was more creation-centred and affirmative of the natural world than that of Rome and of later Catholicism and Protestantism. I have argued this point particularly with regard to the debate between Pelagius and St Augustine of Hippo in the late fourth century.[17] Yet, one has to say that on the basis of early documents from Iona which have only just become available in modern English translations and been subjected to scholarly analysis, we cannot apply this generalization to the Columban Church. The overwhelming themes of the *'Altus Prosator'*, as we have seen, are the fall of creation and the judgement of God. Nature is portrayed not in positive 'green' terms but rather as a wild and terrifying power from which humans need to be protected. Nor is there any trace of a Pelagian stress on the intrinsic goodness and potential of human nature in these early poems from Iona, some of which may have been the work of Columba himself. Thomas Owen Clancy and Gilbert Markus point out that both the *'Adiutor laborantium'* and *'Noli pater'* are, in fact, deeply Augustinian and anti-Pelagian in their stress on the utter inadequacy of the Christian's own moral strength and their insistence that humans are totally dependent on the grace of God. Indeed, they find this position reflected in many other early Irish texts, leading them to the view that 'there is no support in Irish monastic literature for the claim that there is a uniquely "Celtic" theology of grace which is unlike that of the rest of Latin Christendom'.[18]

If we have to be very careful about identifying Columban Christianity as creation-centred, then we certainly need have no qualms about its God-centredness. The two, of course, are not incompatible but it is the latter which comes across particularly strongly in the early literary remains from Iona. Continual praise of God and his wondrous acts is the central *raison d'être* of a monastic community and it is hardly surprising that the theme of praise, so clearly enjoined in the psalms recited daily by the monks, should bulk so large in the writings of Columba and his successors. The

'*Altus Prosator*' begins as a hymn of praise to the Trinity. As we have already noted, it is rich in cosmological and astronomical detail and to that extent does focus on God's work of creation. Yet although it is lyrical in its evocation of the circling planets and the starry heavens, it makes virtually no reference to the beauties of God's creation on earth. Indeed the theme so often associated with Celtic Christianity of praising God through the beauty of nature is noticeably absent from virtually all the authenticated texts which have come down to us from the Columban Church. This is not to say, of course, that it was absent from its theology but simply that we do not have anything from Iona comparable to the beautiful Welsh praise poems, that distinctive genre which has recently been so lovingly analysed and identified by Donald Allchin and Oliver Davies, nor, indeed, to the delightful poems and prayers from the (predominantly Outer) Hebrides, collected in the late nineteenth century by Alexander Carmichael and published in the *Carmina Gadelica*.[19] In the introduction to the original edition of his collection, Carmichael famously remarked that 'some of the hymns may have been composed within the cloistered cells of Derry and Iona'.[20] There is no denying the considerable antiquity of some of the poems that he transcribed and translated but it seems highly unlikely that any of them came from monasteries within the Columban *familia*, all of which, of course, were without cloisters. Their praise of God seems to have been altogether more heaven-centred.

Reacting against the unhistorical romanticism of Carmichael and his ilk, some modern scholars have become very cynical about Celtic Christianity's supposed love affair with nature. Clancy and Markus, for example, suggest that the lyrical nature poems which they concede are found in some early Irish monastic manuscripts, if not in those from Iona, were the work of cultivated literary teachers and administrators in the large monastic towns — 'the real hermit, living in a damp stone or wooden cell, fasting in hot and cold weather to subdue the flesh, terrified of thunder and lightening as the author of the "*Noli Pater*" evidently was, is not the author of these "nature poems".'[21] They also ironically point to poems evoking the delights of nature written by St Augustine of Hippo, the great opponent of Pelagius and supposed exponent of sin-centred and fall-dominated Roman theology. 'The sheer delight in nature, and the way in which such delight elicits praise of God', they conclude, 'is no more Celtic than Hebrew or Roman-African'.[22]

Personally I think this goes too far in dismissing and debunking a genuine aspect of early Irish and British Christianity which has admittedly been over-romanticized and also over-exaggerated in terms of its distinctiveness from Continental European Christianity in the same period. There is one striking aspect of the outlook of the Columban Church which does seem to point to an underlying sense of the goodness of the natural world as well as to the importance of sign and symbol. I am thinking of the value which seems to be attached to blessings and benedictions. Adomnan's *Life of Columba* is full of references to monks and pilgrims coming to the Saint for a blessing. As Donald Allchin has pointed out in considering the similar prominence given to this activity in many early Welsh Christian poems 'to bless (*benedicere*) in its original meaning is to speak good things, to declare the goodness which is latent in the world around us, when that world is seen and known as the world of God'.[23]

The emphasis of the Columban Church on benediction was part of a much wider appreciation in Celtic society of the power of the spoken word. Both blessing and cursing were regarded almost as physical actions which had the effect of transmitting good or evil. In Book 2, Chapter 16 of his *Life*, Adomnan tells of how Columba drove out a devil hiding in a milk pail by making the saving sign of the cross over it. He also upbraided the young man carrying the pail for not having made the sign of the cross before he poured the milk in. We seem here to be in the realm of superstition, pagan charms and incantations to ward off the evil one. Or are we rather in the more mysterious realm of sacramental theology where language and symbol are seen as having a transformative power to realize the presence of Christ and turn evil into good? Again and again Columba is portrayed by his early biographers as averting evil, whether in the form of the Loch Ness monster, a wild boar, an outbreak of plague or a storm at sea, by making the sign of the Cross, raising his hands in blessing and evoking the presence of God.

The theme of deliverance from danger looms large in many of the miracle stories associated with Columba. It is a dominant theme in two of the poems written on Iona which may well have come from his pen — '*Noli Pater*' with its heartfelt prayer to God to avert fire, thunder and lightening and *'Adiutor laborantium'* with its portrayal of the author as 'a little man trembling and most wretched, rowing through the infinite storm of this age'. We are reminded here of just how nasty, brutish and short life could be in the British Isles in the sixth and seventh centuries. In this context, it was not surprising that God's protective powers should be especially stressed. He was seen in an almost literal sense as the shield and defender of those who called on him in faith. St Paul's famous list in Ephesians 6.14-16 of the protective armour available to Christians — the breastplate of righteousness, the shield of faith, the helmet of salvation and the sword of the Spirit — inspired a whole genre of Irish prayers and poems, the most famous of which is that known as 'St Patrick's Breastplate' ('I bind unto myself today the strong name of the Trinity'). Alongside this *lorica* tradition (so called from the Latin word for breastplate) there developed another of encircling prayers, which grew out of the old pre-Christian *caim*, and involved a circle being described around the person, family, community or place which was being entrusted to God's enfolding love. There was a strong physicality about both these styles of prayer, just as there was in Columba's action in blessing the milk churn.

This strong emphasis on the protective power of God, and so by analogy on the protective efficacy of prayer and of his Saints, was part and parcel of a world view which saw evil manifesting itself in definite physical form. Once again, the influence of St Paul, with his evocation of 'principalities and powers ... and the spiritual hosts of wickedness in the heavenly places' (Ephesians 6.12) is very evident. This is graphically brought home in the story in Adomnan's *Life* (Book 3, Chapter 8) in which Columba, praying alone on a wild part of Iona, saw 'a line of foul, black devils armed with iron spikes and drawn up ready for battle' which he realized were preparing to attack the monastery. 'Though he was alone against such an army of countless opponents, he was protected by the armour of St Paul and flung himself into a great conflict.' The battle continued all day until 'the angels of God came to his aid' and helped drive the devils off the island. They were only banished as far as Tiree, however, where they attacked the monks of Mag Luinge with a deadly plague, the effects of which were mitigated by prayer and fasting.[24]

This dramatic account of a cosmic battle between devils and

angels in which Columba took part and which resulted in such physical effects as plague takes us to the third theme which I have highlighted alongside praise and protection as characterizing the theological outlook of the Columban Church — that of presence. We are back once again to the New Testament world of angels and devils so vividly described by Paul and the author of Revelation. We are also not far from the world of pre-Christian Celtic mythology which was full of supernatural happenings and other worldly apparitions. If we are to believe his early biographers, Columba himself was particularly aware of supernatural presences. Adomnan noted 'how great and special were his experiences of angelic visits and heavenly lights'.[25] Those around him regularly saw the Saint himself surrounded by hovering angels or a halo of bright light. Alongside these visions, the members of the Columban *familia* had a highly developed sense of the close presence of the heavenly host. For them the notion of the communion of saints was no empty phrase but a vital doctrine which expressed the nearness of those who had departed from this world and passed to the next. God's protective care encompassed the dead as well as the living and his presence could be felt throughout heaven and earth, as well as across that blurred and narrow line that divided them.

There was another dimension to this theme of presence in the Columban Church. It developed what I think might be described (though not by Columba and his followers who very sensibly eschewed such jargon) as an ecclesiology of presence. Indeed, I suspect that presence might be a better word than mission to encapsulate the heart of Columba's understanding of the role and purpose of the church. We have already seen that he may well not have seen himself primarily as a missionary and that the sources are conflicting as to how often and how far he went out from Iona to preach and evangelize. Much of his time seems rather to have been spent on the island guiding the monks and receiving, blessing and counselling visitors. This emphasis on pastoral care seems to have characterized the Columban Church as a whole. It practised a ministry of presence, witnessing to the Lord not just by rushing around proselytizing and preaching but simply by being there, available when it was needed. A major element of this ministry was the hospitality offered on Iona, symbolized by the washing of visitors' feet by the monks. It also involved a good deal of listening and a good deal of quiet and patient healing of broken souls. The Iona community seems to have offered pastoral care not just to the many visitors who came to the island from far afield but also to the local population. This seems to have been a general characteristic of Irish monasteries. Even an ultra-sceptic about Celtic Christianity like Wendy Davies concedes that the pastoral outreach to the local community in terms of baptism, burial and spiritual counselling was almost certainly stronger in the Christian communities of Ireland, Scotland and Wales than in Continental monasteries. Indeed, she is even prepared to accept that this may even count as a distinct characteristic of Celtic Christianity as a whole.[26]

The practice of this ministry of presence was closely bound up with the central role accorded to penitence in the Columban Church. Many of those who found their way to Iona were misfits, inadequates and outcasts, consumed with feelings of guilt, remorse and low self-esteem. Often they had committed serious crimes for which they could not forgive themselves. On the island they experienced the healing power of the *medicamenta penitentiae*, a combination of penitential discipline and spiritual counselling. We are not talking here about an almost mechanical device of confession and absolution such as the sacrament of penance became in the later medieval church. Rather Columba and his contemporaries had a deep understanding of the human predicament of alienation, self-doubt and separation from God and from other people. They responded with a programme of healing which tackled the whole person, body, mind and soul, and which was predicated on the need for repeated forgiveness and assurance of acceptance by God.

Penitential discipline was far from being soft. The Irish Penitentials, which form the largest single category of document to have come down to us from the golden age of Celtic Christianity, are full of severe punishments for what often seem to our eyes trivial lapses and faults and enjoin a constant state of watchfulness and rigorous self-control. They belong, of course, to a monastic context and it should not be forgotten that they apply first and foremost to those who have taken vows and are living voluntarily under a strict rule. The principle of penitence spread out beyond the monastic *vallum*, however. Much of the work of Columba and his fellow monks on Iona seems to have involved handing out *medicamenta penitentiae* to lay visitors who came in desperate search of healing and wholeness. This could be very harsh. An Irishman called Lugaid who had slept with his own mother was told that he must spend twelve years among the British, 'repenting with tears of remorse', and never return to his native land. Other penitents were regularly banished to Tiree for seven years to live as anchorites, a term which interestingly comes from a Coptic word meaning displaced persons who have lost their place in society.

Harsh though it undoubtedly was, the strong penitential discipline administered by the Columban Church also had great healing power. Hugh Connolly, author of a fine recent book on the Irish Penitentials, describes them as 'handbooks for confessors or physicians of souls who used them in order to steer the faithful away from behaviour which was spiritually harmful, to heal them from the effects of sin, to instruct them in the virtues which were to be sought after and to indicate a means by which this virtuous state might be achieved'.[27] Sensitive pastors that they were, Columba and his contemporaries combined prescription, instruction, advice and empathy in seeking to cure sick souls. Crucial to their approach was the role of the *anamchara*, or soul friend, that distinctive creation of Irish monasticism which combined the roles of spiritual counsellor, father confessor and buddy. Annoyingly, Columba's various biographers give virtually no indication of the Saint's dealings with his own *anamchara* although they tell us enough to make it clear that he had one and that he himself acted in that capacity for others. The rule associated with his name also alludes to the practice when it enjoins monks to perform their vigils 'from eve to eve under the direction of another person'. There is no doubt that the system of soul friends operated within the monastic community on Iona. Unfortunately we can be less sure how far it was extended to the local community and to visitors.

Penitence was also about the propagation of justice and the righting of wrongs. The regime prescribed for penitents was not just designed to address their guilt but also to help their victims and provide reparations for injuries suffered. Here we get a glimpse of Columba as judge, administrator and upholder of law and order as well as priest and pastor. We are, indeed, reminded of his wider political interests and his strong commitment to the rule of law and the replacement of feuding chieftains and warlords by more settled and peaceful systems of authority. Under both its founder and his successors, Iona played a key role in supporting and legitimizing the rule of just and fair monarchs and in promoting the institution of kingship. It was very much a community in touch with secular society and not just a secluded sacred ghetto keeping its distance from the nasty world of politics. At the same time it was also very much a provisional community, avoiding both the triumphalism and the institutional paralysis that comes with building up rigid permanent structures. The ministry of presence that to some extent defined the ethos of the Columban Church did not make it a static body. Rather it was a church that was constantly on the move, physically as well as spiritually. Monks on Iona did not take a vow of stability as their counterparts in Benedictine houses did. Many seem to have served as itinerant clergy going round the country equipped with the basic tools of their trade — Gospel book, psalter, prayer book, hand bell and portable altar.

Provisionality was very much the hallmark of Columban ecclesiology. There were no stone buildings on Iona, nor indeed in the Irish and British monasteries as a whole. Ninian's decision to build a stone church at Candida Casa at Whithorn was exceptional, as Bede noted in his history. Like most of their contemporaries, Columba and his monks were content to worship God in a simple wooden church, a wattle and daub hut or in the open air at the foot of a cross. There was no sense of building a monument that would last for centuries as the Romans had done and the Normans were later to do. In this provisionality we perhaps find another distinguishing characteristic of Celtic Christianity as a whole, identified by Ian Finlay in his life of Columba: 'A Roman saw every achievement in terms of a stone monument, whereas a Celt barely understood the idea of a monument at all ... The Roman bent nature to his purposes, the Celt adapted himself to nature'.[28]

We are brought back to the theme of pilgrimage which we have already encountered in looking at the reasons for Columba's journey to Iona in 563. The Columban Church was a pilgrim church, a community and movement rather than an institution or establishment. It sat lightly to the world, behaving as one who had no abiding city here. Pilgrimage was closely linked with penitence. Surveying different models of penance, Hugh Connolly takes what he calls 'the pilgrimage model' as 'the most quintessentially Celtic':

*All of life is seen as a form of pilgrimage. It is precisely along
this life path that each Christian must make his pilgrim's
progress ... Recognizing that every Christian must, in some
sense, experience a 'wandering in the desert' before attaining
'the promised land', it becomes apparent that he must be
equipped mentally and spiritually to survive the desert ordeal
... The penitentials are really the handbooks of the desert
experience. In this model, the minister is viewed above all
as fellow-traveller, fellow-pilgrim, fellow-sufferer, or to use
the Celtic term, anamchara (soul-friend). The emphasis in
this model is predominantly one of solidarity. Both minister
and penitent are, ultimately, pilgrims on the same pilgrim
path. The important thing is to persevere, to remain steadfast,
to stand ready and even to do battle with the forces of evil.*[29]

Several different elements went into the motif of pilgrimage
that perhaps provides the best key for unlocking the distinctive
ethos and character of the Columban Church. There was the influence of the desert fathers with their austere and ascetic disciplines as they sought to distance themselves from worldly comforts and distractions and find God in the wilderness. There was
the sense of life as a journey, of the need constantly to be prepared to discard unwanted and outdated baggage and to change,
progressing through harms and dangers. There was the emphasis
on white martyrdom and witnessing to Christ through a life of
self-abandonment. There was, too, the strong feeling of community, solidarity and companionship in suffering so that, in
Connolly's words, 'the emphasis is placed not so much on the
saving judgement or salutary medicine but on the fraternal witness and compassion of the *anamchara*'.[30] There is much here that
pre-echoes modern theology in its concern with patripassianism,
God's sharing in the suffering of the world, and its insistence that
it is only the wounded healer who can bring real wholeness to the
broken. Columba and his contemporaries never felt that their spiritual journeys had ended in this world, nor that they had reached
their destinations. They felt themselves and the church which they
built up but did not idolize, to be provisional, imperfect, ever
travelling on to new ways of expressing and understanding the
Gospel and new glimpses of God's glory. This sense is beautifully encapsulated in an old Irish poem attributed to Columba

but almost certainly from a later hand which weaves together the themes of pilgrimage, presence and protection:

The path I walk, Christ walks it.
May the land in which I am be without sorrow.
May the Trinity protect me wherever I stay,
Father, Son and Holy Spirit.
Bright angels walk with me — dear presence — in
every dealing.
In every dealing I pray them
that no one's poison may reach me.
The ninefold people of heaven of holy cloud,
the tenth force of the stout earth.
Favourable company, they come with me,
so that the Lord may not be angry with me.
May I arrive at every place, may I return home;
may the way in which I spend be a way without
loss.
May every path before me be smooth,
man, woman and child welcome me.
A truly good journey!
Well does the fair Lord show us a course, a path.[31]

Notes

1 George Campbell, 8th Duke of Argyll, *Iona*, p.41
2 Donald Meek, review of IONA: The Earliest Poetry of a Celtic Monastery' in *New Blackfriars*, no. 76 (1995), pp.467-68
3 Wendy Davies, 'The Myth of the Celtic Church' in Nancy Edwards and Alan Lane (eds), *The Early Church in Wales and the West* (Oxbow Books, Oxford, 1992), p.11
4 Jocelyn Toynbee, 'Christianity in Roman Britain', *Journal of the British Archaeological Association*, no.16 (1953), p.24
5 Thomas Owen Clancy and Gilbert Markus, *IONA*, p.8
6 Sally Foster, *Picts, Gaels and Scots* (Historic Scotland & B.T.Batsford, London, 1996), p.83
7 Archie Duncan, *Scotland: The Making of the Kingdom* (Oliver and Boyd, Edinburgh, 1975), p.66
8 Thomas Owen Clancy and Gilbert Markus, *op.cit.*, p.222
9 John Ryan, *Irish Monasticism* (Four Courts Press, Dublin, 1992), pp.410-11
10 *Ibid.*, p.409
11 The Rule of Columcille as printed in the appendix of Samuel Stone, *Lays of Iona and Other Poems* (Longmans, Green & Co., London, 1897), pp.112. (An English translation of the Rule can also be found in Edwin Sprott Towill, *The Saints of Scotland* (St Andrew Press, Edinburgh, 1983), pp.50-51)

12 *Ibid.*, p. 110
13 *Ibid.*, p. 112
14 This point is expanded in my book *The Power of Sacrifice* (Darton, Longman and Todd, London, 1995), pp.146-49
15 Ian Bradley, *The Celtic Way* (Darton, Longman and Todd, London, 1993), Chapter 5 *passim*
16 John Ryan, *op.cit.*, p.307
17 Ian Bradley, *The Celtic Way*, pp.62-66
18 Thomas Owen Clancy and Gilbert Markus, *op.cit.*, p.80
19 On the Welsh tradition of praise poetry see Donald Allchin, *Praise Above All: Discovering the Welsh Tradition* (University of Wales Press, Cardiff, 1991) and Oliver Davies, *Celtic Christianity in Early Medieval Wales* (University of Wales Press, Cardiff, 1995). The most accessible edition of the *Carmina Gadelica* is the single volume published by Floris Books in 1992
20 Alexander Carmichael, *Carmina Gadelica* (Floris Books, Edinburgh, 1992), p.30
21 Thomas Owen Clancy and Gilbert Markus, *op.cit.*, p.90
22 *Ibid.*, pp.92-93
23 Donald Allchin, *op.cit.*, p.6
24 Adomnan of Iona, *Life of St Columba*, pp.211-12
25 *Ibid.*, p.233
26 Wendy Davies, *op.cit.*, p.15
27 Hugh Connolly, *The Irish Penitentials* (Four Courts Press, Dublin, 1995), p.21
28 Ian Finlay, *Columba*, p.167
29 Hugh Connolly, *op.cit.*, pp.177-78
30 *Ibid.*, p.178
31 Oliver Davies and Fiona Bowie, *Celtic Christian Spirituality: An Anthology of Medieval and Modern Sources* (SPCK, London, 1995), p.38

5

The legacy of Columba

Columba's influence did not come to an end with his death in 597. Indeed in many ways he became an even more important figure in death than he had been in life. Thanks to the expansion of the monastic *familia* centred on Iona into eastern and southern Scotland and northern England, and the steady growth of the political power of the kingdom of Dál Riata, the cult of Columba flourished during the seventh and eighth centuries. Armies carried his relics into battle as talismans to secure victory while the invocation of his name or prayer through him was said to avert danger. Miracle stories testified to his posthumous powers of protection.

The development of the cult of Columba can be traced very clearly through the successive eulogies and lives produced in the century following his death. These become steadily more hagiographical in tone. Thomas Owen Clancy and Gilbert Markus have helpfully compared the lament composed by Dallán Forgaill, the *'Amra Choluimb Chille'*, just a year or two after his death with the poems written by Beccán mac Luigdech fifty years later. While both authors stress Columba's noble upbringing and asceticism, the latter makes much more of his power to protect those who call on him from danger. Beccán sees the Saint's posthumous power as deriving from his position in the hierarchy of heaven. Yet although he is highly placed with God, he is seen not as a distant figure but as an intimate companion through life's difficulties and dangers. Adomnan, writing around 690, took the cult even further by describing posthumous miracles performed by Columba, including some which he had witnessed himself. Not even contact with the relics of the Saint was necessary to invoke his protective powers. It was enough to mention his name in the context of prayer or praise. One of Adomnan's stories recounts how a group of men, 'wicked and bloodstained from a life as brigands, were protected by songs that they sang in Irish in praise of St Columba and by the commemoration of his name' when the house in which they were gathered was surrounded by their enemies. While they were able to escape unhurt 'through flames and swords and spears', those of their number who had refused to join in the singing perished in the attack.[1]

It is significant that the cult of Columba was developed and encouraged primarily by his successors on Iona. The monastery which he had founded there remained the hub of the extensive and growing Columban *paruchia* in Ireland and Scotland during the two centuries following his death. Columba's successors as abbots of Iona, the great majority of whom were members of his own family, maintained the high and exacting standards that he had set. Writing in the 730s, Bede noted that they were 'distinguished for their great abstinence, their love of God, and their observance of the Rule ... They diligently practised such works of religion and chastity as they were able to learn from the words of the prophets, the evangelists and the apostles.'[2]

In addition to their pastoral and priestly work, the monks of Iona continued the tradition established by the founder of pursuing scholarship and artistic craftsmanship. The community produced two leading cosmographers, Fergil who went to Austria in 742 and became known as the Virgil of Salzburg, and Dicuil who wrote a book on world geography entitled *On the Measurement of the Earth*. The art of manuscript illumination blossomed with the production of the *Book of Durrow* in the late seventh century and the *Book of Kells* a hundred years later. Another kind of craftsmanship, probably imported from Ireland, was displayed in the intricate carving on the faces of the great stone crosses erected in honour of St Martin of Tours and St John.

The artistic influence of Iona spread far across the Scottish mainland. It is largely thanks to the archaeological evidence of stones decorated by carvings of Celtic crosses with their distinctive outline and knotwork that we can be fairly certain that Christianity came to much of Pictland in the 150 years following Columba's death. Members of the community on Iona played a key part in the evangelization of northern and eastern Scotland along with other British and Irish missionary monks like Ternan and Maelrubha. By Adomnan's time there were churches in Aberdeenshire and Angus associated with the Columban *familia*. Bede is clear that Iona ruled the Pictish monasteries and a modern historian of early Scotland, Alfred Smyth, is equally certain that Columba's foundation provided the parent culture for Pictish Christianity and that 'Iona acted as the great disseminator of ideas and motifs throughout Pictland'.[3] Royal patronage almost certainly greatly helped this process. There is evidence that by the late seventh century the kings of Dál Riata had extended their rule eastwards from modern Argyllshire to take in areas of central Scotland previously under Pictish control.

It was also royal patronage that directly brought about the most important extension of the Iona *familia*. Columba's own king-making activities may well have laid the foundations for the mission to Northumbria which was to provide northern England with its own set of Celtic saints. It is certainly striking that, in the words of Ian Muirhead, 'Iona's most successful enterprise came, not through self-initiated mission but through a royal invitation'.[4] The story began with the escape to Iona of the young Anglian prince Oswald in 617 when his father was ousted from the Northumbrian throne. During his sojourn on the island, which seems to have lasted seventeen years, he received not just sanctuary but also instruction in the Christian faith and he was baptized there. In 634 Oswald succeeded in wresting back the Northumbrian throne after fighting a battle against the Welsh king Cadwollan who had seized it the previous year. According to Adomnan, during the night before the battle Oswald had a vision of St Columba who promised him his protection and prophesied that Cadwollan and his forces would be routed. Duly victorious, one of Oswald's first actions on becoming king of Northumbria was to ask Ségégne, the abbot of Iona, to send him a missionary bishop to establish a church in his extensive kingdom which stretched from the banks of the Forth to Yorkshire. The choice fell on Aidan, a saintly figure, who founded his first monastery on the island of Lindisfarne, strategically situated near the royal stronghold of Bamburgh but also remote enough to be a place of prayer and retreat.

Under the ultimate authority of Iona and very much part of the Columban *paruchia*, Lindisfarne became the base for the evangelization of Northumbria and also for much of eastern and central England. It spawned a large number of daughter houses including those at Whitby, Coldingham, Lastingham and Melrose. Bede noted that, in the wake of Aidan, many monks from Scots Dál Riata came 'into Britain and to those English kingdoms over which Oswald reigned, preaching the word of faith with great devotion'.[5] They included the first two bishops of Mercia, Diuma and Cellach. Aidan also trained native Northumbrians for work among the Angles, among them two brothers still remembered in English church dedications — Chad who established his base at Lichfield, and Cedd who worked among the east Saxons and set up monasteries at Tilbury and Bradwell-on-Sea. Perhaps the best known of the products of this branch of the Columban monastic empire was St Cuthbert whose career, in the words of Alfred Smyth, 'represented a happy marriage between older Celtic and newer forms of Anglo-Saxon Christianity in northern Bernicia'.[6] Born in the Borders, he entered the monastery at Melrose in 651 and moved to Lindisfarne as prior in 664, spending the last thirty-three years of his life combining the running of a busy and complex island monastery with periods of solitary retreat and prayer, just as Columba had done a century earlier.

The extension of the Columban Church into Northumbria seems to have coincided with a low point in the fortunes of the kingdom of Dál Riata. Indeed, the two events may be connected. The Strathclyde Britons, rulers of Dál Riata, faced an increasingly hostile challenge from their southern neighbours, and accepted Northumbrian protection and overlordship from around 637. It seems quite likely that the arrival of monks from Iona in Lothian and Northumbria was connected with this new political arrangement. Expansion into the lands of the Angles was to bring its own problems for the Columban Church in the form of direct confrontation with the more Romanized church which had developed in the south of England in the aftermath of St Augustine's mission to Canterbury in 597. This was the background to the Synod of Whitby, at which representatives of each church met to debate their differences. Oswald's brother Oswy, who had succeeded him on the Northumbrian throne in 642, had married a Kentish princess, Eanfled, who had been brought up in Roman ways. Specifically she was accustomed to celebrating Easter according to a relatively new calendar which had been adopted in Rome in place of the old one which was still in use on Iona and in many parts of northern Ireland. This had unfortunate consequences at court. In the words of Bede, it sometimes happened that 'the king had finished the fast and was keeping Easter Sunday, while the queen and her people were still in Lent and observing Palm Sunday'.[7] Wishing to end this anomaly and secure a single agreed method for calculating Easter which would pertain throughout his kingdom, Oswy called a synod at Whitby in 664. The main protagonists were Colman, abbot and bishop of Lindisfarne on the Columban side, and, on the Roman side, Wilfrid, abbot of Ripon who had trained at Lindisfarne but had subsequently visited Rome and converted to its practices.

The debate at Whitby was recorded in detail by Bede. Much of the argument hinged around the authority of Columba and showed the extent to which his example was still being appealed to more than 150 years after his death. Wilfrid began his case by maintaining that the new way of calculating Easter was accepted by the church not just in Rome but in Africa, Asia, Egypt, Greece and everywhere else except among the *Scoti* 'and their accomplices in obstinacy, I mean the Picts and the Britons, who in these, the two remotest islands of the Ocean, foolishly attempt to fight against the whole world'. Colman retorted that it was inconceivable that 'our most reverend father Columba and his successors, men beloved of God, who celebrated Easter in the same [old] way, judged and acted contrary to holy scriptures, seeing that there were many of them to whose holiness the heavenly signs and the miracles they performed bore witness'. Having no doubt that they were saints, he went on to express his clear intention never to cease from following 'their way of life, their customs, and their teaching'. Wilfrid responded by patronizingly describing Columba and his followers as misguided and ignorant men 'who in their rude simplicity loved God with pious intent', and then produced the trump card which is always used to support the Roman Church's claim to supremacy: 'Even if that Columba of yours — yes, and ours too, if he belonged to Christ — was a holy man of mighty works, is he to be preferred to the most blessed chief of the apostles, to whom the Lord said, "Thou art Peter and upon this rock I will build my Church"?'[8]

This appeal to Petrine authority seems to have won the day. Oswy ruled in favour of the Roman method of calculating Easter and also declared his desire that the Northumbrian church should follow Rome in other matters of ecclesiastical order and usage which differed from Irish practice, the most noticeable of which was the way in which monks cut their hair. Colman resigned his abbacy and see and returned to his native Ireland with a number of the monks from Lindisfarne. The Easter controversy dragged on for several more decades. Adomnan was converted to the Roman system of dating in 688 but could not persuade the monks on Iona to join him. Some historians have suggested that he wrote his *Life of Columba* to prove his Columban credentials and his attachment to the founder in the hope that this might persuade the Iona community that it was not a matter of disloyalty to abandon his way of doing things in this particular instance. The extent to which Iona's stubborn refusal to break with tradition led to increasing isolation was highlighted around 717 when the Pictish king Nechtan expelled members of the Columban *familia* from his territories and announced that from henceforth the church in Pictland would follow Roman practices. He was probably motivated partly by his desire to keep in with Northumbria and also under the influence of an English monk, Egbert. About the same time, and possibly as a response to Nechthan's ban, the *paruchia Columbae*, together with most other monasteries in northern Ireland, finally gave up their long cherished traditions and adopted the Roman method of calculating Easter and the Roman style of tonsure.

The Synod of Whitby has often been seen as marking a turning point in the history of Christianity in the British Isles. It is very tempting to interpret it as signalling the crushing of the gentle, anarchic spirit of Celtic Christianity by the authoritarian bureaucracy of the Roman Church, and to some extent Bede's account encourages this temptation. In her book *The Celtic Alternative*, Shirley Toulson argues that 664 was a more important date in British history than 1066.[9] In reality, the significance of the Synod itself was limited although it is certainly true that it symbolized the way things were going for some of the distinctive features of the Columban Church. The key question which divided proponents of Irish and Roman church organization was whether Britain should have a federation of monastic *paruchiae* or a diocesan system run by bishops. This was not on the agenda at Whitby and does not seem to have been discussed at the Synod. Here, however, as over the dating of Easter and the favoured hairstyle for monks, the writing was on the wall for the Columban way of doing things and for a church which looked increasingly provincial and conservative in its ethos. In the opinion of the distinguished historian, Ian Cowan, the church in Scotland was 'consistently moving onwards towards a diocesan system from the eighth century onwards'.[10]

Meanwhile a more immediate threat to the Columban Church, and especially to the primacy of Iona within it, had arrived in the form of an external enemy far more evil-intentioned and deadly than Rome. In 793 Lindisfarne was pillaged in the first recorded Viking attack on the British mainland. Iona suffered the same fate nine years later and in 806 a Viking raiding party savagely slew sixty-eight members of the community. The island was now too vulnerable to remain as the centre of the Columban *familia* and most of the monks from Iona followed their abbot, Cellach, in moving to a new monastery which had been built at Kells in County Meath in the centre of Ireland well away from any danger of attack. A few remained to brave the Viking raids which led to further bloodshed, most notably in 825 when a monk called Blathmac was brutally murdered for refusing to reveal the whereabouts of Columba's shrine. Most of Iona's treasures, including illuminated manuscripts and metalwork, were removed to Kells which gradually achieved primacy within the Columban *paruchia*. Significantly, its abbots continued to style themselves abbots of Iona. With the sea no longer a safe highway but rather a dangerous barrier to communication, Iona became increasingly cut off from other Columban foundations and the centre of gravity within the *familia* shifted to Ireland.

Faced with the common danger of Viking invasion, the Picts and Scots gradually buried their differences and were forced into a closer relationship during the ninth century. The man generally credited with bringing them together and with being the first ruler of a joint Scottish-Pictish kingdom, Kenneth Mac Ailpín, was of mixed descent, his father coming from the ruling family of Dál Riata, the mac Gabráins, and his mother being a Pictish princess. King of Dál Riata from 840 and of the Picts from 843, he went on to achieve ascendancy over the lands around the Tweed which had formerly been part of the Anglian kingdom of Bernicia. By marrying his daughter to the king of Strathclyde he also came to exercise considerable influence over the fourth major ethnic and tribal grouping in North Britain. Thanks to his own Dál Riata background, Kenneth Mac Ailpín was a fervent devotee of Columba and as the first ruler of what was to become the united kingdom of Scotland he gave a considerable boost both to the Saint's cult and to his church there at a time when it was at a low ebb. Perhaps his major contribution lay in moving those of Columba's relics which had not already gone to Kells to Dunkeld in Perthshire which now became the ecclesiastical capital of the new Scottish-Pictish kingdom. This happened in 849.

In death, as in life, Columba was enlisted in the cause of dynastic rivalries and political battles. Rivalry between Picts and Scots was not ended with the rule of Kenneth Mac Ailpín. His successors as kings of Alba gradually extended their control over the more northerly Pictish territories, helped, in the words of Sally Foster, by 'the aggression of a revitalized Gaelic Church, promoting the language of St Columba'.[11] A carved stone near Forres dating from the late ninth or early tenth century, which seems to commemorate a significant victory of the Scots over the men of Moray, perhaps one of the last outposts of Pictland, has a scene showing a Mac Ailpín king being crowned apparently in the presence of St Columba and St Andrew. Columba's crozier, or staff, was carried as a protective device by Scottish armies facing the invading Viking armies in the tenth century. In a similar way his psalter, which had been taken to Ireland along with other relics, was encased in a silver casket and paraded by the Uí Néills in all their military adventures. The O'Donnells, successors to the Uí Néills, became hereditary keepers of the *Cathach*, which was believed to secure victory in battle, and they continued parading it until the sixteenth century.

Columba's growing cult status as a protector of kings and guarantor of military victory helped to assure Iona of a continuing role throughout the tenth and eleventh centuries even though it had ceased to be the centre of the monastic *familia*. It was during this period that the island became the recognized burial place for kings. Altogether forty-eight Scottish monarchs are said to have been interred there, together with four from Ireland and eight from Norway, this last group being a pointer to the considerable Nordic cult which developed around the figure of Columba in the late tenth century. The half-pagan Norsemen saw the Saint of Iona as having many of the qualities of the Viking war-god Odin, and took Columban Christianity to Iceland and Greenland.

The church on Iona also received a boost from Queen Margaret of Scotland who seems to have been instrumental in ordering the construction around 1080 of the first permanent stone place of worship, and the earliest of the surviving ecclesiastical buildings on the island, St Oran's Chapel. In other respects, however, Queen Margaret was not a friend to the Columban Church and its continuing survival as a distinctive entity in Scotland. The rule of her husband, Malcolm Canmore, which lasted from 1058 to 1093, is generally taken to mark the anglicizing and Romanizing of the Scottish church, a process in which Margaret is traditionally credited with playing a key role. Unable to speak Gaelic, she introduced many English customs and practices to the Scottish court and relied heavily for ecclesiastical advice on her chaplain, Turgot, who had been sent to Scotland by Lanfranc, Archbishop of Canterbury. Possibly under his influence, the Norman system of territorial diocesan organization already in place in England was introduced north of the border. Scottish monasteries, including those recently set up by the reforming Culdee movement from Ireland, were reorganized along Continental lines. Margaret was behind the foundation of the first Benedictine monastery in Scotland which was established at Dunfermline Abbey in 1072. Benedictine monks were to establish an abbey on Iona in 1200, effectively ending more than 600 years of a distinctive Columban church presence.

In Ireland, as in Scotland, the Columban Church largely disappeared as a distinct entity during the twelfth century. An attempt by Derry to assert its supremacy within the Columban *familia*, which probably lay behind the mid-twelfth century Irish *Life* of the Saint, was one of the last expressions of the old monastic-based church. Following the Norman invasion of Ireland in 1169, the monasteries throughout the country were brought under episcopal control and, like other similar federations which crossed diocesan boundaries and owed allegiance to an abbot rather than a bishop, the Columban *paruchia* disintegrated. The territorially organized diocesan system which St Patrick had first tried to introduce seven centuries earlier had at last prevailed. Patrick's own star was also in the ascendant as the see which he had established at Armagh was recognized as having primacy in the Irish church as a whole and his position secured as the nation's patron saint. Attempts to promote Columba's candidacy in his native land came to naught, not least because the power of his main supporters, the northern Uí Néills, was in decline.

The new nation of Scotland might well have been expected to adopt Columba as its patron saint. Certainly his stock remained high long after the particular style and structure of church with which his name had been associated had disappeared. In 1123 a major monastery dedicated to him was founded on the island of Inchcolm in the Firth of Forth. From it comes the *Inchcolm Antiphoner*, one of the most important manuscripts in the history of plainchant which contains a remarkably beautiful service of commemoration for St Columba. It includes some antiphons, with an altogether freer and more ethereal sound than that of Gregorian chant, which some musicologists feel may belong to the seventh or eighth century and take us back to the sound of Christian worship around Columba's own time.[12] Another fine piece of art associated with the Saint is the Monymusk Reliquary, also known by its Gaelic name 'Breccbenach', a small wooden oratory decorated with bronze and silver plates, semi-precious stones and enamels. Apparently built to house a bone relic of Columba, it was entrusted to the abbot of Arbroath by King William I of Scotland so that it might be available for blessing the royal troops in battle. On the eve of the decisive battle in 1314 when Robert the Bruce confronted the English army under King Edward II of England at Bannockburn, the reliquary was paraded before the Scottish forces and fully lived up to its reputation as a bringer of victory.

Yet despite the extent of his cult and his enlistment by successive kings as protector and patron, Columba was not to become Scotland's patron saint. In a recent book, Ursula Hall has shown how the rival cult of Andrew probably began in Scotland in the late eighth or ninth century among the Picts of north east Fife, having spread from Northumbria where it had been strongly championed by Wilfred, the chief protagonist of the pro-Roman side at the Synod of Whitby. There is some suggestion that Andrew may have been favoured by the Picts as a counter to the Scots' support for the Gaelic Columba. There was certainly a geographical dimension to the contest between the two saints' supporters. While Columba reigned supreme in the west, Andrew's cult spread in the east from its original base at Kinrymont, the site of the modern city of St Andrews. As the centre of ecclesiastical gravity gradually shifted eastwards, first from Iona to Dunkeld and then to St Andrews, so the apostle gained ground over the Irish monk. Queen Margaret of Scotland gave a boost to the cult of St Andrew by establishing a ferry crossing across the Forth for pilgrims visiting his supposed relics at Kinrymont. It was many centuries, however, before Andrew rather than Columba was universally recognized and indubitably established as Scotland's patron saint. His popularity rose slowly but steadily throughout the Middle Ages, helped by the emergence of the Archbishopric of St Andrews with undisputed jurisdiction over a single independent Scottish ecclesiastical province.[13]

Even if he did not become its patron saint, Columba remained a significant spiritual influence in Scotland. His standing was not seriously diminished by the Reformation. Indeed, numerous Presbyterian and Episcopalian churches have been dedicated to him. Like St Patrick in Ireland, he has appealed as much to Protestants as to Roman Catholics. Even the ultra-Calvinistic 'Wee Frees' in the Free Church of Scotland have enthusiastically claimed him as a mentor and traced their own roots from the church that he founded on Iona.

It could, indeed, be argued that it is among the Protestant communities of the Highlands and Islands that the distinctive precepts of Columban Christianity have been most clearly and closely followed in recent centuries. Donald Meek has characterized 'Highland religion' as involving 'a profoundly serious approach to worship, an awareness of the centrality of Scripture, respect for preaching, the observance of the Sabbath and an overall awareness of the sovereignty of God'. He points to the central place of the psalms in worship, respect for supernatural experience and 'a pervasive sense of another level of existence'. He also mentions a traditional emphasis on oral transmission of information, song and story which has produced 'a massive capacity for memorization, harnessed skilfully by catechists and preachers', and an innate conservatism and capacity for retrospection leading to 'a natural tendency to admire the leaders, models and practices of an earlier age', especially the heroes of both the Christian and pre-Christian past.[14] With the possible exception of the strict Sabbath observance, all of these were strong characteristics of Columban Christianity. There is a distinct echo of Columba's mixture of deep piety, genuine humility and strong, if somewhat autocratic, leadership qualities in the make-up of that formidable spiritual élite known as 'The Men' who wielded such influence in Highland and Island Presbyterianism during the eighteenth and nineteenth centuries. Like the Saint of Iona, they combined a sensitive awareness of the supernatural, a deep prayerfulness and a strong personal charisma with a powerful regulatory role in the local community, directing the overall religious, moral and social tone of their localities. Some were said, like Columba, to possess gifts of prophecy.[15]

The legacy of Columban Christianity is particularly clear in the rich and distinctive body of Gaelic religious verse produced in the Highlands in the eighteenth and nineteenth centuries. The *Dain Spioradail* (spiritual songs) and *Laoidhean Spioradail* (spiritual hymns) written by Dugald Buchanan of Perthshire, Peter Grant of Strathspey, John MacDonald of Ferintosh and other evangelical Presbyterians and Baptists exhibit several of the characteristics that we have already noted in the verses of Columba and his successors on Iona. There is the same stress on the sovereignty and majesty of God, displayed through his works in creation and illustrated through the vivid physical imagery of the Psalms, on the importance of neighbourliness and community, on God's protective powers and the utter dependence of humanity on Him, and above all on the theme of spiritual pilgrimage. The subjects covered in Buchanan's eight surviving compositions, which were intended as a systematic theology to be sung by the people, echo those of the *'Altus Prosator'* and other early works from Iona: the greatness of God; the sufferings of Christ; the Day of Judgement; the dream; the Christian hero; the skull; winter; prayer.

These evangelical Highland poets shared the conviction so strongly held in the Columban Church that faith should be sung as well as spoken, expressed in poetry rather than prose and communicated through symbol, image and metaphor as much as through concept, reason and argument. Their work also involved a similar intermingling of the sacred and the secular, the eternal and the everyday. The verses of these spiritual bards were sung at winter ceilidhs and at summer gatherings in the hill shielings or shelters. Their lifestyles, too, often echoed those of Columba and his fellow monks. Many regularly retreated to their own private places of prayer in the hills, like the late eighteenth century bard of Harris, Iain Gobha (Iain the Blacksmith) who wrote his verses after many hours of wrestling with the Almighty in his 'cell' amidst the rocks on which he had carved the simple words 'God is love'. It is significant that John Macinnes, author of the standard work on Highland evangelicalism, should acknowledge Columba as 'the first of the Gaelic spiritual bards'.[17]

Traces of this deep and distinctive Columban spirituality are still clearly discernible in the Christian life and witness of the Presbyterian communities in the Western Isles, although they have sadly been overlaid by a harsh judgmentalism and narrow legalism which derive from Calvinism and other later extraneous influences. I suspect that it may well be in the utterly God-centred worship of the Gaelic-speaking congregations of the Church of Scotland, the Free Church and the Free Presbyterian Church in its stark simplicity and, to modern mainland taste, its rather severe and forbidding austerity that we get closer than anywhere else today to the spirit of worship on Columba's Iona. Instead of the buzz of idle chatter which precedes most church services nowadays, there is an almost palpable stillness as worshippers take their places up to twenty minutes or so before the start of the service simply to sit in silent prayer and contemplation without any visual or aural distraction, both musical instruments and decoration or ornament of any kind being barred from church buildings. There is a severity here that even Columba might find a shade austere but there is also an atmosphere of profound awe and reverence before the mystery of God, undisturbed by the cloying chords of keyboards or the relentlessly upbeat syncopation of praise bands, that I think he would recognize and appreciate. He would also feel at home with the sung parts of the service, consisting as they do exclusively of unaccompanied chanting of the psalms. Gaelic metrical psalmody, with its mournful and deeply moving cadences which seem to rise and fall in time with the rhythm of the sea, bears certain clear resemblances to the descriptions given of the chanting of psalms by the early monks on Iona. It is also uncannily similar to the style of psalm singing still practised in the Coptic Church in Egypt and Ethiopia. Could it be that preserved in the remote extremities of ancient Christendom, in the eastern and far western Celtic fringes which we know were once so closely linked, are the remnants of a once universal Christian chant which may well have derived from the synagogue and have been used by Our Lord himself in his own worship?

If the Protestant churches of the northern part of the Outer Hebrides may in some ways be the most faithful, if also perhaps the most reluctant inheritors of Columban Christianity, their Catholic neighbours in the southern isles remain close to its gentler and more immediately attractive side. In such places as South Uist and Barra, the sense of supernatural presences has survived untrammelled by Calvinistic distrust and rationalism and there is more interweaving of the sacred and the secular with singing and dancing not being frowned upon as they are in the more northerly islands. It is significant that it was predominantly from the inhabitants of these southern isles that Alexander Carmichael collected the Gaelic prayers, blessings, charms and incantations that went into his *Carmina Gadelica*. I have already expressed my own doubts about his claim that some of this material went back to Columba's time. It seems to me to represent a later strain of Christian spirituality, altogether less severe and ascetic and more affirmative of the natural world. It is, indeed much more congenial to the modern mind than the somewhat gloomy and doom-laden verses which have come down to us from sixth- and seventh-century Iona. The contents of the *Carmina Gadelica* have, of course, been widely popularized and taken up in recent years. This is wholly to be welcomed. Their use in both public and private devotion is enormously refreshing and reinvigorating for the corporate and individual spirituality of many contemporary Christians. Their strong affirmation of the goodness and sacredness of the natural world is providing a badly needed corrective to the anti-physical bias which has so long predominated in the thinking and preaching of the western church. While they are to be commended in every way, however, I am not sure that we can see them as following in a direct line of descent from the verses of Columba's church with their darker and more penitent tone.

It is rather to the Inner Hebrides that we need to look to find the most faithful and also the most fruitful and forward-looking working out of the legacy of Columban Christianity today. Appropriately, indeed, it is on the island where the Saint himself settled that for the last half century or so a Christian community has been engaged in a life of prayer, work and involvement in the world in which the themes of presence, poetry, politics, pilgrimage and penitence are all to the fore. Today's Iona Community is of course an essentially modern creation — indeed, it stands as one of the most innovative and creative expressions of Christian living in the twentieth century. It is not a self-conscious re-creation of Columba's original monastic community, nor does it follow in the same unbroken and largely unconscious 'Celtic' tradition as the continuing Christian communities of the Western Isles. Its Columban character is rather in large part the consequence of the particular outlook and personality of its founder, a twentieth-century saint who bears a quite extraordinary resemblance to the man who first established a Christian community on Iona 1400 years earlier.

Like Columba, George MacLeod came of upper-class stock, being the son of a baronet and Conservative MP. Educated at Winchester and Oxford, he retained a certain patrician manner and tone of voice throughout his life. He also retained a fondness for the monarchy. A Scottish socialist with whom I recently watched the film 'Sermon in Stone', in which he narrates the story of the Iona Community, was struck by the fact that the clear high point for him was showing the Queen round the newly restored Abbey buildings. In another parallel with Columba, he rejected a career in military or political service in favour of the church, serving as a parish minister first in Edinburgh and then in depressed inner-city Glasgow, where he conceived the idea of rebuilding the Abbey on Iona with a mixture of unemployed workmen and trainee ministers. MacLeod was forty-two when he began his project on Iona in 1938, exactly the same age that Columba is popularly portrayed as being when he first set foot on the island in 563. He shared his predecessor's combination of deep prayerfulness and humility, imaginative insight and poetic flair and charismatic leadership qualities accompanied by a somewhat autocratic and dominant manner. Shamelessly exploiting his aristocratic contacts, he persuaded his friends in high places to part with their money much as Columba had persuaded kings and princes to give land and endowments for his monastic foundations. In its early days the all-male Iona Community was run like a boys' public school with cold swims before breakfast and a strict regime in the dormitories at night. Columba would have been at home with this ascetic atmosphere just as he would have warmed to the deep pastoral instincts of a man who regularly took bottles of champagne to one of his poorest parishioners who was dying of cancer. He would also surely have recognized in MacLeod's superbly crafted prayers the distinctive voice of the Gaelic poetic imagination.

The Iona Community of the late 1990s, like the Iona community of the late 590s, remains strongly influenced by the character and the causes of its founder. Just as the abbots who followed Columba continued his passionate commitment to king making and church planting, so George MacLeod's successors have carried on his fight for nuclear disarmament, the ending of poverty and environmental exploitation, and the dismantling of denominational barriers. In both cases, the agenda set by an exceptionally charismatic, strong-minded and imaginative founding father has continued to be followed after his death. This is not to say that the two men have received similar posthumous treatment. George MacLeod's bust may stand in a prominent place in the Iona refectory but there is no sign as yet of the development of a cult such as that which built up around his sixth-century predecessor. Ron Ferguson's biography of George MacLeod can perhaps at one level be compared to Adomnan's *Life of Columba*, the life of the community's founder being written by one of his successors as leader, but it is not a work of hagiography. If MacLeod emerges from its candid and enthralling pages on the side of the angels, it is not from any sycophancy on the part of his biographer who reveals a deeply human character, with all the flaws and imperfections of the species, if also a more than usual measure of almost childlike goodness and purity. In a telling passage which makes a direct comparison with his subject's illustrious predecessor, Ferguson writes, 'he is not a saint in the conventional sense though he is in the sense that Columba was — an outrageous, volatile adventurer, taking God at his word'.[18] MacLeod's relics are unlikely to be paraded before any Tartan Army in the struggle for an independent Scotland, although his spiritual banner has flown high over the peace camp at Faslane.

The Iona Community manages in a unique way, I think, to combine the more difficult and off-putting aspects of Columban Christianity with its more immediately appealing themes and to integrate them in an approach to living the Gospel which is thoroughly contemporary. It does not shirk from the penitential and judgemental strain, applying it both to individual self-examination and to the corporate sins of injustice and exploitation committed in an increasingly divided world. At the same time it maintains an attitude of openness to all human conditions and needs, a remarkable creativity in worship and a determination to find and proclaim the presence of God in the ordinary and everyday things of life. If the specific areas singled out for special attention by Community members in the late 1990s — sharing communion, justice, peace and the integrity of creation, racism and interfaith, the rediscovery of spirituality, the cause of the poor and exploited, constitutional issues, and work with young people — did not feature on the agenda of the monks on Iona in the late sixth century that is largely because they would have taken most of them for granted. It is a measure of how far we have departed from earlier Christian principles that these causes now need to be specifically flagged up and championed.

Of course, there is a danger of overstating the influence and legacy of Columba, conscious or unconscious, on the modern-day Iona Community. It is emphatically not in the business of reconstructing or returning to some imagined golden age in the island's past. Indeed, I am glad to say that the Community's commitment to the rediscovery of spirituality explicitly includes as one of its objectives 'exposing the frequent romantic misunderstandings about the nature of Celtic spirituality'.[19] Yet the benign, if searching, presence of Columba hovers over many of the Community's distinctive precepts and practices. It is particularly evident, perhaps, in the monastic character of the five-fold rule to which the two hundred or so members commit themselves: regular prayer and Bible study on both an individual and communal basis, sharing and accounting for the use of money (including giving away a tenth of personal disposable income); planning and accounting for the use of time; meeting with and accounting to one another (shades of the soul friend but with this function being performed by groups rather than individuals); and working actively to promote justice, peace and the integrity of creation.

As in Columba's time, much of the work of the Iona Community takes place off the island itself. Its members live and work across the British Isles with some further afield. There are Columban houses in several locations providing little colonies of prayer and sanctuary for the bewildered and bruised and several projects running in Glasgow where the Community's administrative centre and leader are based. The well deserved reputation of the Wild Goose Resource and Worship Groups for innovative and creative liturgical reform takes its members into churches the length and breadth of the British Isles and beyond to enthuse congregations and lead worship workshops. The heart of the Community, however, remains on Iona where a small core of resident staff, supplemented by a constantly changing band of volunteers staying for a few months or so, minister to a host of visitors, guests and pilgrims. It is here that the legacy of Columba is most evident. Iona remains first and foremost a place of prayer and worship. The daily office of the modern community is at once a less dominant and much grander feature than it was for the monks of the sixth and seventh centuries. Instead of meeting five times during the day and night in a small wooden building, the Community now meets for worship just twice, at 9 am and 9 pm, in the spacious surroundings of the restored Benedictine Abbey. The services, like the setting, would almost certainly strike Columba as very elaborate. The old concentration on chanting the psalms has given way to much more varied ways of praying and singing God's praise, though the singing on Iona is still often unaccompanied. As for the early monks, worship is integrated with work and is seen as encompassing the daily chores that need to be performed around the place as well as making time for periods of individual prayer and reflection. To underline this, the morning service does not end with a benediction but rather with responses which prepare those present to go straight out to the life of the world, there to continue to worship in the context of their work. For the same reason the evening service does not begin with a call to worship, 'for we have been at worship all day long'.[20]

Like Columba and his monks, those who live in and around Iona Abbey today exercise an important pastoral ministry to the island's many visitors. I have heard modern Iona dismissed by its detractors simply as a mecca for 'spiritual tourism'. It is true that many of those who make the short crossing from Mull probably fall into the category of tourists but there is a very thin dividing line between tourism and pilgrimage. Among the island's day visitors, and even more among those who book in for a week at the Abbey or the MacLeod Centre (a residential centre opened in 1988 particularly to cater for young people and families) are many bearing pain, nursing grievances or troubled with doubts and anxieties. Members of the resident community reach out to these pilgrims and penitents and seek to help them towards healing and wholeness. Their names can be added to those whose needs are regularly remembered by the network of intercessors who form the Community's prayer circle. They are also invited to bring their brokenness before God in the healing service which takes place in the Abbey every Tuesday evening. Here they can experience the laying on of hands without any of the razzmatazz or hyped-up expectations associated with some other contemporary healing ministries. At Iona no promises are made about miracle cures or sudden deliverances. What is offered is simply a way of experiencing God's everyday work of bringing wholeness to His broken people. In addition to this special focus on healing there is also a constant ministry of hospitality.

Poetry, image and symbol are as important on Iona today as they were 1400 years ago. Perhaps one of the most creative pieces of symbolism is enacted when the Wednesday pilgrimage reaches the beach where Columba is thought to have landed in 563. Those taking part search for a stone which they throw into the sea as an act of physically casting off unpleasant aspects of their lives or memories of which they wish to rid themselves. At the same time, each person is often invited to pick up another stone to take home and keep as a reminder of a new commitment made. The liturgies which have been produced by the Iona Community are richly poetic in their rhythms and imagery and have already done much to enliven the rather prosy and plodding language of worship in so many churches. Perhaps the Community's most notable contribution to the poetry of worship has been in the field of hymnody. The songs which have emanated from the Wild Goose Resource and Worship Groups, and particularly from the pens of John Bell and Graham Maule, have justly achieved widespread popularity for their vivid imagery and their engagement with contemporary issues. Significantly, several of them have focused on the Columban theme of presence, most notably perhaps the song 'Faces of God' which begins 'God who is everywhere present on earth'.[21] The doctrine of presence does, indeed, provide the Iona Community with what is perhaps its most distinctive theological emphasis, as articulated in the preface to its *Worship Book*:

> *Our whole life, we believe, is a search for wholeness. We desire to be fully human, with no division into the 'sacred' and the 'secular'. We desire to be fully present to God, who*

is fully present to us, whether in our neighbour or in the
political and social activity of the world around us, whether
in the fields of culture or of economics, and whether in prayer
and praise together or in the very centre and soul of our
being.[22]

Those other key themes of Columban ecclesiology —
provisionality, pilgrimage and penitence — are also very much to
the fore in the life of the contemporary Iona Community. Indeed, the first is underlined in its very title which suggests a view
of church as community or movement rather than fixed organizational structure. Like Columba and his followers, members of
the Iona Community do not see themselves as belonging to a distinct church or denomination. They continue to belong to their
own home churches. Those visiting the island for whatever length
of time are encouraged to go back to their own churches, renewed
and refreshed in their commitment. The Community itself moves
in and out of particular projects depending on where it sees the
needs as greatest and its resources as strongest. One constant is a
passionate commitment to fight against injustice and violence in
the world, if necessary by direct political and social action. As in
Columba's time, Iona is not a place of isolation or withdrawal
from society's problems. The Community has no time for a view
of spirituality as 'an exercise in pietistic individualized detach-
ment' but sees it rather as 'a multi-faceted engagement or
centredness in the life of the Spirit, with a clear social dimension
and expression.'[23] Just as Columba's determination to work for
order and justice led him to intervene in councils and conven-
tions and champion the new institution of kingship against the
rule of warlords and robber barons, so his successors on Iona
today involve themselves in campaigns for fair trade, full employ-
ment and constitutional reform. The recent burial on the island
of John Smith, Labour Party leader and devout Christian socialist,
recalls Iona's former role as the final resting place of prominent
public figures.

Iona is almost certainly a more exuberantly joyful and relaxed
place to be now than it was in Columba's time. The Community
bubbles with life and creative energy, its songs proclaiming that
'the life of the world is a joy and a treasure' and inciting us to
'Dance and sing, all the earth'.[24] Today there are no gloomy
penitentials prescribing punishments for every conceivable lapse.

This does not, however, betoken a lack of awareness of or an in-difference to the numerous hurts that need to be healed, the sins that need to be forgiven, the wrongs that need to be righted and the disorder and imperfection that needs to be redeemed in the modern world. The Community lives under the shadow of Christ's Cross just as it prays and works under the shadow of the high-standing crosses dedicated to St Martin and St John which domi-nate the approach to the Abbey. Its joy never slips into triumphalism, nor its relaxed spirit into complacency. It remains uneasy about the deep stain of sin that sullies the world. It is con-stantly mindful of the presence in our midst of the weak, the vul-nerable and the marginalized and names them before God, not with a sigh of resignation or despair but with a sense of determi-nation to work for a better world and hasten the coming of Christ's kingdom. It is this deep spirit of penitence, summed up in the song, 'We lay our broken world in sorrow at your feet', which is for me the most authentic mark of the continuing presence of Columban Christianity on Iona.[25]

Notes

1   Adomnan of Iona, *Life of St Columba*, p.111
2   Bede, *The Ecclesiastical History of the English People*, p.115
3   Alfred Smyth, *Warlords and Holy Men*, p.79
4   Ian Muirhead, 'The beginnings' in *Studies in the History of Worship in Scotland* (eds. Duncan Forrester and Douglas Murray) (T & T Clark, Edinburgh, 1996), p.5
5   Bede, *op.cit.*, p.114
6   Alfred Smyth, *op.cit.*, p.33
7   Bede, *op.cit.*, p.153
8   *Ibid.*, pp.155-59
9   Shirley Toulson, *The Celtic Alternative* (Century Hutchison, London, 1987), pp.10-11
10 Ian Cowan, 'The Post-Columban Church' in *Records of the Scottish Church History Society*, no.18 (1974), p.259
11 Sally Foster, *Picts, Gaels and Scots*, p.113
12 On the music of the *Inchcolm Antiphoner*, see John Purser, *Scotland's Music* (Mainstream Publishing, Edinburgh, 1992), pp.39-45. The Lauds for the Feast of Columba have been recorded by Capella Nova on CD.
13 Ursula Hall, *St Andrew and Scotland* (St Andrews University Library, St Andrews, 1994)
14 Donald Meek, typescript of pamphlet on religion in the Highlands to be published in the World Council of Churches Gospel and Culture series, pp.26-27.
15 See Chapter 2, note 18
16 There is an excellent article on 'The Men' by Donald Meek in the *Dictionary of Scottish Church History and Theology* (T & T Clark, Edinburgh, 1993), pp.558-59

17   John Macinnes, *The Evangelical Movement in the Highlands of Scotland 1688 to 1800* (Aberdeen University Press, Aberdeen, 1951), p.265

18   Ronald Ferguson, *George MacLeod* (Collins, London, 1990), p.421

19   *What is the Iona Community?* (Wild Goose Publications, Glasgow, 1996), p.14

20   *The Iona Community Worship Book* (Wild Goose Publications, Glasgow, 1991), p.7

21   This song can be found in John Bell and Graham Maule, *Heaven Shall Not Wait* (Wild Goose Publications, Glasgow, 1987) and also in *Songs of God's People* (Oxford University Press, Oxford, 1988), No. 36

22   *The Iona Community Worship Book*, p.7

23   *What is the Iona Community?*, p.14

24   'Oh the Life of the World' by Kathy Galloway can be found in *The Iona Community Worship Book*, p.11 and *Songs of God's People*, No. 87. 'Dance and Sing' by John Bell and Graham Maule is in *The Iona Community Worship Book*, pp. 12-13 and in *Heaven Shall Not Wait*.

25   'We lay our broken world in sorrow at your feet' by Anna Briggs is in *Songs of God's People*, No. 113.

6

The journey on —
politics, penitence and pilgrimage

On what journeys are Christians being led 1400 years after Columba's death? Do the particular themes which characterized his life and thought have any relevance now or do they belong to a long lost 'primitive' age which it is quite futile to try and recapture in our high-tech, multi-choice 'advanced' society?

On the basis of what we know of Columba from his early biographers, it is tempting to say that those following most faithfully in his footsteps in late twentieth-century Britain are the dwindling band of monarchists and the growing army of charismatics. King making, as we have seen, was one of his main activities, springing from a deep attachment to the institution of monarchy and a concern with the promotion of social justice and order. Columba supported the cause of princes and kings and invested them with authority and legitimacy through Christian ritual because he felt that they offered a fairer and more settled pattern of government than the arbitrary rule of tribal chieftains and warlords. The monarchy stands at a low ebb in contemporary Britain. Columba surely calls us to greater loyalty and respect for the institution, not out of slavish sycophancy but because of its Christian character and its clear identification with the values of public service, personal sacrifice and national unity. The churches have a particular role in the rehabilitation of the royal family and in helping to develop a new model of monarchy which will serve as a symbol and focus of unity and shared values in our increasingly fragmented and divided country.

The wider agenda which underlay Columba's king-making also has considerable relevance today. There is a global trend towards tribalization and narrow ethnic nationalism from which Britain is not immune. Injustice, violence and abuse of power are just as prevalent now as they were in sixth-century Ireland. Through his own example Columba calls the church to be political and prophetic, not by making easy moralistic statements but by costly engagement in the world.

As well as being a politician and prophet, Columba was, if we are to believe his early biographers, a miracle worker and faith healer forever making contact with angels and foretelling the future — the very model, indeed, of a modern charismatic. The only gift of the spirit that he is not portrayed as possessing is that of speaking in tongues. Charismatic renewal has been one of the most significant growth areas in church life across all denominations over the last few decades. It is significant that several leading charismatics have recently written highly affirmative studies of Celtic Christianity and identified strongly with what they take to be its Spirit-led character.[1] It is undeniable that Columba and his contemporaries were much more open to the supernatural and much less rationalistic and earth-bound in their faith than most western Christians are today. They seem to have had much in common with contemporary charismatics in matters both of practice and belief, whether it is in the cross vigil which they adopted for prayer with arms outstretched and palms raised heavenwards or the stress on spiritual warfare with the forces of evil personified and seen in almost physical terms. To those of us who are not charismatics, this aspect of Columba's Christianity may not be particularly appealing, any more than his king-making activities will be to many today, but we cannot ignore something that was so central to him. One of the undoubted benefits of the modern charismatic movement is the extent to which it has broken down denominational barriers. In this, of course, it is also standing in the tradition of Columba who had no sense of belonging to a particular church. From before the long and weary centuries of ecclesiastical empire building and narrow denominationalism he calls us back to ecuminism.

I intend in the remainder of this last chapter to return to the three trinities of themes which I identified in Chapter 4 as characterizing Columban Christianity and consider their relevance to the church today. To provide a contemporary context for that discussion I want first briefly to invoke another trio which describe the prevailing social and cultural climate: postmodernism, privatization and plurality.

Postmodernity has been described as the fragmentation of modern western culture and the celebration of the particular. It goes along with the collapse of overarching values and the privatization of public institutions, leading to an erosion of the notion of the common good and a retreat into narrow and selfish individualism. With the aid of new technology, many people are withdrawing increasingly from shared social activity and leading ever more private lives. The seemingly unstoppable march of the free market produces ever greater consumer choice, a baffling and bewildering situation which is the antithesis of true freedom, being created by powerful commercial pressures and largely unavailable to the growing ranks of the poor. The 'me society' encouraged by these developments is characterized by greed and incoherence, as well as by the moral relativism and lack of consensus inherent in a culture of pluralism.

It seems to me that Columban Christianity stands in almost total opposition to all of these trends which are so clearly evident in contemporary Britain. It has become fashionable to see Celtic Christianity as squaring with postmodernist pluralism. In our pick-and-mix culture people are increasingly assembling their own personal spiritual packages in which elements of the Celtic tradition are combined with some New Age nostrums and other bits and pieces. Celtic poems and prayers, reproduced on attractive cards and in beautifully produced little books, are becoming the totems of this new privatized religion. Who needs to go to church or to join in any corporate activity when you can worship in the comfort, privacy and cocooned isolation of your own home with a handful of prayer cards, paperbacks and tapes? I hope that I have already said enough in this book to make readers realize that this kind of approach is the antithesis of Columban Christianity. It envisaged the church first and foremost as community. Monasteries, themselves supreme expressions of the corporate life, were grouped together into families to give even more emphasis to this communal dimension. Of course the Columban monastery was also a place for retreat and private prayer. It provided a balance between individual and corporate worship which was part of that rhythm of life which pervaded Irish monasticism. In the life of the Columban Church as a whole engagement in the world was as important as withdrawal from it. So was costly self-sacrificial discipleship. It could hardly be further from our current culture of narcissism.

There is another aspect to the cultural make-up of contemporary Britain which perhaps makes us closer to the age of Columba than to more recent periods of our Christian past. Our society is often described as post-Christian or secular. It is certainly highly materialistic. In many ways, indeed, we are considerably less spiritually aware than our pre-Christian Celtic ancestors who had a highly developed religious faculty and a clear belief in the value of the human soul, the reality of an afterlife and the existence of a power beyond themselves. How can Christians today begin to communicate the good news of the Gospel to people who are not simply ignorant of the basic principles of the faith but have lost touch with the religious and spiritual dimension of life, having been brutalized by the new 'paganism' of the National Lottery and the mobile phone, the tabloid press and breakfast television, designer drugs and alcoholic soft drinks? If we are indeed entering another Dark Age, may it not be appropriate to look again at those institutions which shone the beacon of Christian hope and enlightenment across our benighted land so many centuries ago? Perhaps the model of the Columban monastery, with its openness, hugely varied activities and strong community orientation offers beleaguered churches and congregations a way forward into the next millennium.

If we are to explore this model seriously, we would do well to start with that trio of prayer, psalmody and poetry which I have suggested formed the devotional base of Columban monasticism. Prayer, it almost goes without saying, is at the heart of Christian life. Yet we know how difficult it is amidst the pressures and distractions of modern life to get into a rhythm of praying regularly. It is noticeable that more and more Christians are discovering the benefits of saying a daily office, either on their own or with others. Another characteristically monastic form of prayer is also experiencing a comeback as people of all faiths join those without clearly articulated beliefs in vigils for peace, for political prisoners and for people with AIDS. Keeping vigil can be one of the most powerful ways of expressing solidarity with those who are broken and bringing them before God, not least when it is done, as it was by Columba, through the long slow watches of the night.[2]

Another welcome development in the worship of many churches is the growing prominence given to the psalms. Although there is a long way to go before they are restored to the central place they occupied in the liturgy of the early church, throughout the Middle Ages and in the aftermath of the Reformation, we are at least more ready to use those that speak of anger, despair and doubt as well as the more familiar hymns of praise and reassurance. The Iona Community's Wild Goose Resource and Worship Groups have taken a leading role here with publication of *Psalms of Patience, Protest and Praise*. We need more generally to rediscover the poetic quality of Columban spirituality. Worship in most churches is too long-winded, too cerebral and too conceptual — in short, too prosy. We try to pin God down instead of approaching him through our imaginations by means of poetry, song and symbol. Many of the new liturgies which have replaced the resonant if dated language of the sixteenth and seventeenth centuries have fallen down because they lack real poetic quality. One of the richest blessings that the revival of Celtic Christianity is bringing to the Church is a marvellous stock of prayers, new and old, which have the twin virtues of brevity and genuine poetic quality. We are also beginning to realize that in communicating the Christian message story telling is as valid as preaching, and weaving a narrative as important as expounding a complex theological point. This is not to say that the quest for theology should stop, nor that we should cease wrestling with deep and difficult questions. Far from it — but this too can be done through poems and images as well as by argument and concept.

Maybe Columba has another message for modern theologians in the form of a gentle reminder of the principle of *lex orandi, lex credendi*. His own study was rooted in a life of prayer and devotion and not carried out in the detached academic atmosphere of a university department of divinity. His theology sprang naturally out of his attitude of praise in which the mystery of God was approached with an almost childlike sense of wonder and an intense respect as well as with a delight in the marvels of creation. One only has to compare the opening verse of the '*Altus Prosator*' with the matey familiarity of so many modern worship songs to see how thin and trite our notion of praise has become.

We badly need to recover the Columban sense of praise in all its fullness and richness. We have stripped wonder out of most experiences, including in much modern worship out of our encounter with God. A culture where everything is 'up front' and instantly accessible as well as instantly available leaves little room for mystery and holiness. When there is so much cynicism and negativity around, it is very important to have praise which is proclaiming the essential goodness of God's creation. There is also a great need to foster those qualities of awe and anticipation without which the human spirit cannot grow and develop. So many features of modern life seem threatening, whether it be technology, insecurity, addiction, crime and violence, or just the speed of change, that we need more than ever the blessings and benedictions which formed such an important part of Columban theology. We also need to recover a sense of the strength of God's protective and enfolding love. Celtic prayers of protection speak powerfully to many who find themselves lost or hurt in today's brutal and stressful world. During a period as part-time chaplain at a psychiatric hospital, I myself found them particularly meaningful for those suffering from depressive illness and schizophrenia. The use of prayers in the *lorica* (breastplate) or *caim* (encircling) traditions may, indeed, have distinct therapeutic value in the treatment of psychiatric illness. Some people who have experienced drug or alcohol addiction or sexual abuse, are gripped by a sense of demonic possession and the almost physical reality of dark and malevolent forces. In this respect they can relate to the world of Columba and perhaps they can be helped by the kind of prayers that he used to create circles of protection.

Like the idea of protection, the notion of presence is one that could fruitfully be made much more of by contemporary Christians. Its insistence that God is to be found throughout the physical world has obvious environmental and ecological implications. The Columban doctrine of presence also seems to me to provide a helpful ecclesiological model for churches struggling to find a role and identity as we move into the new millennium. We are obsessed with the model of mission nowadays with churches forever being encouraged to undertake mission audits, produce mission action plans and train congregations as missionary cells. This is essentially managerial jargon — witness how no business nowadays seems to be able to operate without a mission statement — and in the words of the ever-perceptive religious commentator, Clifford Longley, 'managerial jargon will not stir our lost sea of faith'.[3] Gillean Craig, an Anglican priest in East London, has recently argued very persuasively against this whole mission-oriented approach in favour of one which is based on the principle of presence. Rather than thinking in terms of missionaries, and so creating a false distinction between Christians and others, she prefers the notion of witnesses:

> *Witnesses are not people radically different from those to whom they witness. Witnesses are people whose experience gives them a story to tell that confronts others with, and helps them to come to a decision about, the truth. Our witnessing can take a wide range of authentic forms, depending on our circumstances, talents and abilities. It ranges from the constant and steady witness of the faithful presence — the people ready to suffer and rejoice with their neighbours, the church still open for prayers and praise — to the dynamism of radical social action, of open-air evangelism and challenging drama. We can be mute witnesses in the holiness of our lives, and vocal witnesses telling others the story of Christ ... There is a whole theology of witness to explore.[4]*

What is being advocated here seems to me to be very close to the ministry of presence practised by the early monks on Iona. I have already argued that Columba may not, in fact, have seen himself as a missionary at all. He would, however, undoubtedly have seen himself as a witness to Christ. Indeed the Greek word for witness, *marturos*, gives us the term martyrdom, which, as we have seen, was central to the Irish monastic culture in which Columba was brought up. Being a martyr does not necessarily mean, just as it did not mean for Columba and his contemporaries, facing persecution and dying for the faith. It does mean constant witness to Christ through life and example. It also means simply being around, as Jesus was, to listen and pray with people, to stand alongside them in their brokenness and help them to wholeness. This unspectacular if intensely demanding and draining ministry of presence may well be one of the most important ways in which the church can serve God and his people today when so many other specialist agencies and professional carers are available only by appointment during office hours.

A church which is engaged in this ministry of presence is more likely than one committed to the more exciting and macho theology of mission to be a penitential community. In Columban theology penitence was bound up with the ideal of martyrdom and with a sense that the Christian must 'die daily' as a way of saying yes to the Cross. If this involved serious self-sacrifice and self-examination, it was not simply a matter of gloomy introspection and suffering harsh penalties when one transgressed. Within the Irish monastic tradition penitence provided a pastorally sensitive way of dealing with the real human problems of sin, guilt and alienation. It was more of an approach and an attitude of mind than a system or mechanism. At its heart was the understanding that forgiveness is available over and over again and that both penitent and priest are pilgrims and soul friends together in a similar condition of brokenness. The model of the wounded healer has rightly become very popular in the fields of pastoral care and counselling. I suspect that there are other aspects of this complex and little investigated area of Columban theology which might prove fruitful and suggestive today.

A church that is more penitential is likely to be more provisional in its outlook and structures. Provisionality is already becoming something of a buzz-word in ecclesiastical circles. We are coming to the end of a thousand-year period, inaugurated by the Normans, of building great solid stone places of worship designed to last for a very long time. Many of our great cathedrals and churches have enormous beauty and are full of poetic symbolism and mystery. Others, however, have become millstones round the neck of congregations whose energies are almost entirely devoted to keeping the roof watertight and the windows vandal-proof. The settings for Christian worship in the future, I suspect, will be more provisional and temporary, more like the simple wooden churches and wattle and daub huts where Columba and his followers met to pray and sing. This will involve a difficult transition in which the church comes to be defined less in terms of its buildings and more in terms of its people, its ideas and its actions. It will involve much painful letting go and jettisoning of organizational and structural baggage as Christians see themselves less as part of a fixed institution and more as members of a community on the move.

It is highly appropriate that the fourteen-hundredth anniversary of Columba's death is being marked by pilgrimages across the length and breadth of the British Isles. For it is as pilgrim people, walking, talking, praying and sharing together that we most clearly carry the legacy of the Columban past into our own Christian futures. Pilgrimage involves journeying back as well as forwards, back not just into the recesses of our own individual souls with their rich store of memories and experiences and their untidy bits of unresolved and unfinished business but also into our collective roots and traditions. Those who do not know where they have come from often have very little sense of where they are going. One of the great malaises in modern British society is that so many people are not in touch with their roots. Through exploring and celebrating the life and thought of Columba and his near-contemporaries in Ireland, Scotland, Wales and England, we are able to connect with a common tradition that has nurtured and influenced nearly all who live in these lands today and which has to some extent made us what we are. We can connect too in a mysterious but meaningful way with the communion of saints, that great and silent company who have gone before us in the faith and with whom we are bound in the one body of the Church, militant on earth and triumphant in heaven.

Saints are not much in vogue in contemporary Christianity. Yet we live in a world full of idols and stars where pop singers, footballers and supermodels are worshipped and iconized far more than any Celtic monk ever was. Maybe we need to be rather more enthusiastic about our saints, old and new. It is worth pondering David Adam's remark that 'a church without saints is a church without heaven' and Cardinal Basil Hume's observation that 'Saints from all ages have something to say to us. Their lives speak eloquently of God. We can be more touched by contact with holy people than by any number of sermons.'[5] In our supposedly egalitarian and politically correct culture it goes against the grain to say that some are more saintly or holy than others. Yet that is how Columba's contemporaries regarded him and it was because of their acknowledgement of his saintliness and their readiness to follow his leadership that he was able to do all that he did for Christ. Were he to come back today, I suspect that he would be put down by colleagues jealous of his advantages of birth and his evident talents, hounded by tabloid journalists determined to dig out the dirt in his past and squashed by committees anxious to maintain the *status quo* and preserve a quiet life. The modern church has opted to be run by management structures rather than led by saints. We prefer setting up working parties to following a prophet.

Perhaps this is Columba's most important and most difficult message for us today. The issue of leadership is an extraordinarily confused one in the contemporary church. Authority in the Columban Church was personal rather than institutional. Most modern churches are increasingly setting up complex institutional structures in an effort to diffuse and decentralize authority. There are good reasons for doing so. The dangers of allowing charismatic leaders a power and influence in the church unfettered by institutional checks and balances were made only too obvious by the recent scandal involving the Sheffield Nine o'Clock service in which exploitative and manipulative leadership went unchecked for too long because of a laxity and lack of authority and control within the hierarchy of the Church of England. Yet have we left any room for leadership in our quest for accountability, decentralization, corporate management and democratic participation? No doubt Columba had a fiercely autocratic side, could be extremely difficult to live with and rubbed some people up the wrong way. Yet ultimately he achieved what he did because he was recognized as a leader and people were prepared to follow him, just as 500 years earlier people had been prepared to follow Jesus of Nazareth. Like Jesus, Columba spoke as one having authority and had a manifest integrity and humility which made people trust him. As we journey on today, could he be urging us to find new leaders and follow them as they follow the One who is Lord and Master of us all.

> *From Erin's shores Columba came*
> *To preach and teach and heal,*
> *And found a church which showed the world*
> *How God on earth was real.*
>
> *In greening grass and reckless wave,*
> *In cloud and ripening corn,*
> *The Celtic Christians traced the course*
> *Of grace through nature borne.*

In hosting strangers, healing pain,
In tireless work for peace,
They served the servant Christ their Lord
And found their faith increase.

In simple prayer and alien land,
As summoned by the Son,
They celebrated how God's call
Made work and worship one.

God grant that what Columba sowed
May harvest yet more seed,
As we engage both flesh and faith
To marry word and deed.[6]

Notes

1   See, for example, Michael Mitton, *Restoring the Woven Cord* (Darton, Longman and Todd, London, 1995) and Ray Simpson, *Exploring Celtic Spirituality* (Hodder and Stoughton, London, 1995)
2   I owe this point to an article by Alan Griffiths on 'Keeping Vigil' in the *Fairacres Chronicle*, vol.28, no.1 (1995), pp.27-33
3   *Daily Telegraph*, 22 September 1995, p.29
4   *Church Times*, 2 February 1996, p.8
5   Quoted in *The Times*, 16 June 1996, p.15
6   Wild Goose Resource Group, 'From Erin's shores' in *Love From Below* (Wild Goose Publications, Glasgow, 1992), p.123

Suggestions for Further Reading

The best full-length biography of Columba remains Ian Finlay's *Columba* published by Victor Gollancz in 1979. There are two superb editions of Adomnan's *Life of St Columba*, edited respectively by A.O. and M.O. Anderson (First edition published by Edinburgh University Press in 1961, Second edition by Oxford University Press in 1991) and by Dr Richard Sharpe (Penguin Books, 1995). Both have very valuable introductions and notes. The full text of the mid-twelfth Irish Life of Colum Cille can be found in Irish and English in Máire Herbert's scholarly study of the history and hagiography of the monastic *familia* of Columba, *Iona, Kells and Derry* (Oxford University Press, 1988).

The most accessible edition of Bede's *Ecclesiastical History of the English Speaking People* is probably that edited by Judith McClure and Roger Collins and published by Oxford University Press in the World's Classics series in paperback in 1994.

An extremely useful collection of poems from seventh- and eighth-century Iona, including '*Altus Prosatur*', '*Adiutor Laborantium*', '*Noli Pater*', '*Amra Choluimb Chille*' and the poems of Beccán mac Luigdec, has been gathered together in their original Latin and Irish versions and translated into modern English with illuminating commentaries and notes by Thomas Owen Clancy and Gilbert Markus in *IONA: The Earliest Poetry of a Celtic Monastery* (Edinburgh University Press, 1995).

The best and most up-to-date general works on the age of Columba are Alfred Smyth's *Warlords and Holy Men: Scotland AD80-1000* (Edward Arnold, 1984) and Sally Foster's *Picts, Gaels and Scots* (Historic Scotland and B.T. Batsford, 1996). The penitential nature of early Irish Christianity is interestingly treated in Hugh Connolly's *The Irish Penitentials* (Four Courts Press, Dublin, 1995). Those wishing to pursue the elusive figure of St Ninian are directed to John MacQueen's *St Nynia* (Polygon, Edinburgh, 1990) and Daphne Brooks' *Wild Men and Holy Places*

(Canongate Press, Edinburgh, 1994). The other Scottish Saints can be looked up in the excellent *Dictionary of Scottish Church History and Theology* (T & T Clark, Edinburgh, 1993) and Edwin Sprott Trowell's *The Saints of Scotland* (St Andrew Press, Edinburgh, 1983).

The influence of Columba on George MacLeod and the Iona Community can be traced in Ron Ferguson's books *Chasing the Wild Goose* (Collins, London, 1988) and *George MacLeod* (Collins, London, 1990) There is a plethora of recently published books on Celtic Christianity and its relevance today. They include Ian Bradley's *The Celtic Way* (Darton, Longman and Todd, London, 1993), Michael Mitton's *Restoring the Woven Cord: Strands of Celtic Christianity for the Church Today* (Darton, Longman and Todd, London, 1995) and Ray Simpson's *Exploring Celtic Spirituality* (Hodder and Stoughton, London, 1995).

The Iona Community

The Iona Community is an ecumenical Christian community, founded in 1938 by the late Lord MacLeod of Fuinary (the Rev. George MacLeod DD) and committed to seeking new ways of living the Gospel in today's world. Gathered around the rebuilding of the ancient monastic buildings of Iona Abbey, but with its original inspiration in the poorest areas of Glasgow during the Depression, the Community has sought ever since the 'rebuilding of the common life', bringing together work and worship, prayer and politics, the sacred and the secular in ways that reflect its strongly incarnational theology.

The Community today is a movement of some 200 Members, over 1,400 Associate Members and about 1,600 Friends. The Members - women and men from many backgrounds and denominations, most in Britain, but some overseas - are committed to a rule of daily prayer and Bible reading, sharing and accounting for their use of time and money, regular meeting and action for justice and peace.

The Iona Community maintains three centres on Iona and Mull: Iona Abbey and the MacLeod Centre on Iona, and Camas Adventure Camp on the Ross of Mull. Its base is in Community House, Glasgow, where it also supports work with young people, the Wild Goose Resource and Worship Groups, a bimonthly magazine (*Coracle*) and a publishing house (Wild Goose Publications).

For further information on the Iona Community please contact:

The Iona Community,

Pearce Institute,

840 Govan Road, Glasgow G51 3UU

T. 0141 445 4561; **F.** 0141 445 4295.

Other Titles available from WGP

SONGBOOKS with full music (titles marked * have companion cassettes)
THE COURAGE TO SAY NO; 23 SONGS FOR EASTER & LENT*John Bell and Graham Maule
GOD NEVER SLEEPS – PACK OF 12 OCTAVOS* John Bell
COME ALL YOU PEOPLE, Shorter Songs for Worship* John Bell
PSALMS OF PATIENCE, PROTEST AND PRAISE* John Bell
HEAVEN SHALL NOT WAIT (Wild Goose Songs Vol.1)* J Bell & Graham Maule
ENEMY OF APATHY (Wild Goose Songs Vol.2) J Bell & Graham Maule
LOVE FROM BELOW (Wild Goose Songs Vol.3)* John Bell & G Maule
INNKEEPERS & LIGHT SLEEPERS* (for Christmas) John Bell
MANY & GREAT (Songs of the World Church Vol.1)* John Bell (ed./arr.)
SENT BY THE LORD (Songs of the World Church Vol.2)* John Bell (ed./arr.)
FREEDOM IS COMING* Anders Nyberg (ed.)
PRAISING A MYSTERY, Brian Wren
BRING MANY NAMES, Brian Wren

CASSETTES & CDs (titles marked † have companion songbooks)
Tape, IONA ABBEY, WORSHIP FROM EASTER WEEK (ed/arr Steve Butler)
Tape, THE COURAGE TO SAY NO † Wild Goose Worship Group
Tape, GOD NEVER SLEEPS † John Bell (guest conductor)
Tape, COME ALL YOU PEOPLE † Wild Goose Worship Group
CD, PSALMS OF PATIENCE, PROTEST AND PRAISE † Wild Goose Worship Group
Tape, PSALMS OF PATIENCE, PROTEST AND PRAISE † WGWG
Tape, HEAVEN SHALL NOT WAIT † Wild Goose Worship Group
Tape, LOVE FROM BELOW † Wild Goose Worship Group
Tape, INNKEEPERS & LIGHT SLEEPERS † (for Christmas) WGWG
Tape, MANY & GREAT † Wild Goose Worship Group
Tape, SENT BY THE LORD † Wild Goose Worship Group
Tape, FREEDOM IS COMING † Fjedur
Tape, TOUCHING PLACE, A, Wild Goose Worship Group
Tape, CLOTH FOR THE CRADLE, Wild Goose Worship Group

DRAMA BOOKS
EH JESUS...YES PETER No. 1, John Bell and Graham Maule
EH JESUS...YES PETER No. 2, John Bell and Graham Maule
EH JESUS...YES PETER No. 3, John Bell and Graham Maule

PRAYER/WORSHIP BOOKS
PATTERN OF OUR DAYS, THE, Kathy Galloway (ed.)
PRAYERS AND IDEAS FOR HEALING SERVICES, Ian Cowie
HE WAS IN THE WORLD, Meditations for Public Worship, John Bell
EACH DAY AND EACH NIGHT, Prayers from Iona in the Celtic Tradition, Philip Newell

IONA COMMUNITY WORSHIP BOOK,
WEE WORSHIP BOOK, A, Wild Goose Worship Group
WHOLE EARTH SHALL CRY GLORY, THE, George MacLeod

OTHER BOOKS
EARTH UNDER THREAT, THE: A Christian Perspective, Ghillean Prance
MYTH OF PROGRESS, THE, Yvonne Burgess
WHAT IS THE IONA COMMUNITY?
PUSHING THE BOAT OUT, New Poetry, Kathy Galloway (ed.)
EXILE IN ISRAEL: A Personal Journey with the Palestinians, Runa Mackay
FALLEN TO MEDIOCRITY: CALLED TO EXCELLENCE, Erik Cramb
REINVENTING THEOLOGY AS THE PEOPLE'S WORK, Ian Fraser

WILD GOOSE ISSUES/REFLECTIONS
WOMEN TOGETHER, Ena Wyatt & Rowsan Malik
APOSTLES' CREED, THE: A Month of Meditations, David Levison
SURPLUS BAGGAGE: The Apostles' Creed, Ralph Smith